compassionate conservatism

What it is
Why we need it

Jesse Norman
Janan Ganesh

© Jesse Norman 2006

Published by
Policy Exchange
Clutha House
10 Storey's Gate
London SW1P 3AY

020 7340 2650
www.policyexchange.org.uk

ISBN 0-9551909-3-2

Printed by Heron Dawson & Sawyer
Designed by John Schwartz, john@thefrontline.net

Contents

Introduction

One of the most prominent themes of the Conservatives under David Cameron has been that of "compassionate conservatism". In a speech at Policy Exchange in June 2005, at the outset of his campaign to be leader of the Conservative party, Cameron said that his party would stand "for compassion and aspiration in equal measure". In December, in his acceptance speech as leader, he called for "a modern and compassionate conservatism which is right for our times and our country". And since then, he and other senior Conservatives have repeated this call in speeches, in the media and in political advertisements; and the theme of "modern, compassionate conservatism" has formed the core of the party's new statement of aims and values, *Built to Last*.

Cameron has described compassionate conservatism in terms of trust, responsibility and inclusiveness:

> *The more we trust people, the stronger they and society become. We're all in this together... we have a shared responsibility for our shared future... There is such a thing as society; it's just not the same thing as the state.*
>
> *We will stand up for the victims of state failure and ensure that social justice and economic opportunity are achieved by empowering people and communities.*

From the outset, however, many media commentators—including Jonathan Freedland and Polly Toynbee of *The Guardian*, Martin Wolf and Philip Stephens of the *Financial Times*, Simon Heffer and Mark Steyn in *The Daily Telegraph*—have expressed scepticism or outright hostility to the idea of compassionate conservatism. But while all are certain compassionate conservatism is deeply flawed, they cannot agree how. For some, it is simply an empty slogan: a bit of rhetoric whose purpose is political rebranding, rather than a deep change of political perspective. For others, it is a contradiction in terms: conservatism and compassion, whatever "compassion" amounts to, are intrinsically opposed and no amount of nice words can reconcile them. For yet others, it is a substantive idea, but the wrong one: insufficiently meritocratic, or too paternalistic, or a disastrous reheat of the "compassionate conservative" electoral slogan of George W. Bush in 1999.

Needless to say, all this disagreement suggests that there may be something here of real interest and importance. But what is compassionate conservatism? What does the contrast between state and society actually amount to? What does compassionate conservatism have to say about the challenges that face Britain today?

These are the topics of this book. Our argument is simple. This country faces two great problems in the 21st Century, a problem of trust and a problem of security. To tackle these problems, we need a vastly better understanding of what British society is and could be. Only a compassionate conservatism, properly conceived, can give us this understanding. When we have it, we can develop radical, effective and wide-ranging new policies.

Two problems

We can see signs everywhere that the social ties between us are weakening: in political disaffection, in social indicators such as rates of drug abuse and single parenthood; in immoveable pockets of inner-city deprivation; in low savings expectations; and in racial and religious discontent. It seems we trust our leaders, our neighbours, our visitors, and even our own future behaviour, less and less.

This we describe as the problem of trust: how do we strengthen our society? The second problem is that of security: how to protect ourselves from threat, be it from terrorism, say, or from loss of energy supplies, or from damage to the environment.

These problems are inextricably linked, for both force us to look inwards and to reconsider the nature of British society. What is striking is how impoverished political debate has become on these issues, and how reliant we are on a single and inflexible model of state provision of public services to solve our social ills. This approach is visibly insufficient to the task, in areas ranging from pensions to education, from housing to welfare provision. The result is that we are running huge social and economic risks, which recent consumer and government spending booms have merely disguised.

What we need is a new vision of society: a humane, principled and long-term intellectual basis for our social renewal. The solution to the problems of trust and security lies in a greater sense of our cultural identity: of what we as Britons are, of our society, of our institutions and values, and of what we have to offer the world. With this in hand, we can see both the opportunity and the pressing need for a huge devolution of power away from Whitehall, towards independent institutions, towards the private and voluntary sectors, and towards local government.

This is what compassionate conservatism can give us. Its compassion is one of fellow-feeling, not of pity: one of identification, concern and sympathy with others, not one of condescension to them. It offers a new way of thinking about society, which can then be a basis for fresh and dynamic policies. This new political vision is both rooted in our national traditions, and recognisably conservative. But it is neither paternalist nor merely economically individualist; and it is entirely different from the conservatism of George W. Bush.

A starting point

In trying to understand compassionate conservatism, however, and its distinctive vision of state and society, we will need to take the reader on a journey. We must begin with what is already familiar, with some practical issues of politics, and then delve into some of the core ideas and assumptions that unconsciously shape our thinking about what to do, before returning to policy.

We start with the state. Is it working? Is it well-suited to the social and economic problems of the 21st century? Can it support us as a nation when we fall sick, when we are out of work or when we retire? Can it educate us and protect us properly? And if it can do so now, can it continue to do so in the future?

This is a starting point that some may find hackneyed. But these are the central political questions of our time. If, as we argue, the state is and will increasingly be under huge risk of failure, then the need to conceive an alternative is not optional for us; it is mandatory, indeed pressing. And it is mandatory not despite, but precisely because, our public services are so important, and because it is so important to enhance and develop them.

A few definitions first, however. "The state" in its fullest meaning includes all the organs of British government, including the Crown, Parliament (the legislature), Whitehall (the executive), local government and the courts (the judiciary). But our own focus is mainly on the parts that implement policy: the executive and local government. That is, it is on Downing Street, on all the departments and ministries of government, on the executive agencies and similar organisations, and on town halls. These are the parts that raise and spend our money. They include the NHS, education, the benefits system, pensions, social housing, and the police.

The present argument is addressed to those who are interested in political ideas and not political labels, be they left or right, who sense that there is something wrong in their lives at present, and who would like to do something about it. What it demands of the reader is a little time—a couple of hours or so—and a measure of fair-mindedness. What it offers is a new way of thinking about an old political problem.

One of our themes is the importance of conversation. In this spirit, readers who would like to contribute ideas, evidence, or arguments of their own, for or against, are encouraged to contact Jesse Norman by email at jesse.norman@policyexchange.org.uk.

AJN
JG
June 2006

1: The state we're really in

IT WAS the best of times, it was the worst of times, it was the age of wisdom, it was the age of foolishness, it was the epoch of belief, it was the epoch of incredulity, it was the season of Light, it was the season of Darkness, it was the spring of hope, it was the winter of despair.

So begins Dickens's *Tale of Two Cities*. Something similar might be said of Britain today. On the one hand, the country is going through an unprecedented period of sustained economic prosperity. Inflation is around 2%, real interest rates have been exceptionally low, and employment is high. Our national output or Gross Domestic Product has grown in every quarter since 1993. If the numbers are to be believed, we have not enjoyed such continued economic success since records began in 1704.

On the other hand, a visitor might rightly ask: if you're so rich, how come you ain't happy? Of course, happiness and well-being are notoriously slippery concepts, which are generally not well served by numerical analysis. But it's hard to deny that something is wrong. The UK has had the highest drug use in Europe for at least ten years, in almost every major category: in cocaine, amphetamines, ecstasy and cannabis. Among the larger European countries, the UK has by far the highest levels of binge drinking, with nearly 30% of all teenagers estimated to have been drunk ten or more times a year. The UK has the worst record for teenage pregnancies in Europe. Our teenage birth rates are twice as high as Germany, three times as high as France and five times as high as Holland. The proportion of children in the UK who are in households without work is the highest in Europe.

These social problems affect different sets of people differently: the poor more than the rich, the sick more than the healthy, those in the

North and in cities more than those elsewhere. Take Scotland, for
instance. There has been a 350% rise in drink-related deaths in the last
two decades. Around 13,000 people die because of smoking related diseases every year. More than a third of Scotland's 12-year-olds are over-
weight or clinically obese. Male life expectancy in parts of Glasgow is
falling, not rising: it now stands at 54 in the district of Calton, 11 years
less than the state pension age.

The different impact of social factors is especially marked between old
and young. Those born in the 1950s—the generation of Tony Blair and
Gordon Brown—found a Britain of relative social cohesion and security. They grew up when the NHS was still basking in its post-war glory,
offering the best healthcare in the world equally to all, and free of
charge. Relatively few enjoyed a university education but those that did
paid nothing, indeed they were subsidised to attend. Jobs came with
secure employment and rewarding pensions based on final salaries. An
average couple could expect to buy their first house in their twenties.
Foreign conflicts stayed foreign. Until the emergence of the provisional
IRA in 1969 there was little threat of bombs on British streets. Crime
was low.

These advantages did not and could not last, and—while it would be
absurd to be dewy-eyed with nostalgia for the 1950s—those growing up
today enjoy few of them now. They will pay towards their university
education. They will be treated by an NHS that has been overtaken in
quality and results by its international peers. They will enter a job market which is ever more internationally competitive. They will have to
change jobs and retrain several times in the course of a lifetime. They will
first buy a flat, not a house, and that in their thirties. They will grow up
in a country where drug abuse is common, and where there is wide-
spread fear of terrorism and violent crime.

It is perhaps not surprising then that popular trust in government is
at a record low. After all, the first duty of government has always been
to protect the people, and this it is increasingly failing to do. Much has
been made of falling voter turnout in British elections since 1997.
What is especially interesting, however, is how this disengagement

splits broadly along the lines of age, ethnicity and income. In the 2005 General Election, only 37% of 18-24 year-olds voted, as opposed to 75% of those over 65. Among those of black or ethnic minority background, 47% voted; among whites, 62% did. Among those categorised in social classes D and E, 54% voted; among those in classes A and B, 70% did. Some commentators have suggested that the problem is that voting is not easy enough. But this mistakes the symptom for the cause. The issue is not how easy it is to vote. It is whether it is worth voting at all.

Of course, there have been improvements in many areas; one cannot have 13 years of unbroken prosperity without that. But even so, it is hard to avoid the conclusion that for many people the basic social contract—the implicit deal by which people trade social engagement for security—is starting to fall apart.

Why has this happened? Those on the left of the political spectrum have attributed this social decomposition to what they see as the selfish individualism and inequality created by Thatcherism. Those on the right have cited, among other things, poor long-term economic management, the growth of permissive legislation in the Wilson years, and the decline of the Church. Our focus, however, is less on causes than on outcomes, and specifically on two crucial questions. Why has British government, with all the panoply of the welfare state, the public services and the police, been unable to make a real impact on these deep social problems? And given that more cash has been spent on the state in recent years than at any time in history, can even its present performance be sustained?

By the end of this book, we will have an answer to the first, deep, question. The second, shallow, question can be answered now, however. The answer is no.

Centralisation and growth
First, however, some political and historical context. Political traditions wax and wane. But one crucial continuity in politics has been the steady growth, in some form or other, of "the state" in this country over the last nine hundred years.

However, it is only after 1945 that the state has assumed its recognisable modern form. Since then, we can identify four broad phases in its development: enlargement in the late 1940s and 1950s, stasis in the 1960s and 1970s, selective retrenchment in the 1980s, and further extension after 1997. Over this period both the main political parties have, with one partial exception, supported this continuing pattern of state growth.

The exception is, of course, Mrs Thatcher. It is hard to recall now how lacking British citizens were in 1979 in the basic economic freedoms that we now take for granted. Huge parts of the UK economy were directly owned by the state, including all or part of the telecoms, water, electricity, coal, steel, shipbuilding, road and air transport and car industries. Wages were restrained by collective agreement between government and the unions, and labour markets were rigid and immobile. The prices of many goods were determined by government fiat, not by market mechanisms. Foreign exchange controls strictly limited the amounts of money that could be brought in or out of the country, and so restricted foreign direct investment. The top rate of income tax was 83%.

This relative economic decline could not continue. In response, Mrs Thatcher rolled back the frontiers of the state. She abolished exchange controls, cut direct taxation, deregulated the City of London in the "Big Bang", broke the power of the unions and freed up labour markets. Her government privatised half of what was known as the "State Trading Sector", and sold off a quarter of the stock of council housing.

But less famously, the Thatcher government also greatly centralised what remained. The deep issue behind the economic decline of the 1970s had been the increasing ungovernability of Great Britain. This showed itself in, among other things, a lack of control over public expenditure. In particular, the rise in spending towards 50% of GDP in 1975-76 precipitated a fiscal crisis and forced the Callaghan government to call in the IMF. Throughout the 1980s Whitehall was desperately seeking to restrain public spending and inflation, and this, plus the increasing demand for central accountability for spending, fed through into greater central control in education, health and policing. The effect was most felt in local government where many local councils spent heavily and raised their rates (and so inflation, since rates were included in inflation calcu-lations), in part for hostile political reasons. In reaction, the Thatcher government imposed central regulation of local spending, pulled more tax powers back to the centre, and capped local rates.

As this potted history brings out, there are two ways in which the state can grow. It can grow economically, quantitatively, in pounds, shillings and pence by taking more of what we produce in taxes every year. Or it can grow socially, qualitatively, in the different ways in which it affects our lives, our goals and projects. A new regulation may have no effect on GDP, but a huge effect on how we live. The state can be extensive, or it can be pervasive, or both.

The Thatcher government reduced the pervasiveness of the state, in ways we have seen. But economically, its extent was almost unchanged between 1979 and 1997, at about 36%-37% of GDP consumed in taxes. Since 1997, however, the state has grown fast in both directions. It is now projected to cost 43% of GDP in taxes in 2010, a rise of about one-fifth in 13 years. This will increase further if, as is widely expected, the over-all tax burden continues to rise. The number of those directly or indi-rectly employed by the state has risen to 6.8 million, or 784,000 more than in 1997.

But it is on the harder-to-measure social, qualitative side that the dif-ference is most marked: the state has become hugely more pervasive since 1997. For example: the government's new Tax Credits do not merely means-test household income, but demand details of household costs in order to pay for people's childcare. The government's Pension Credit was introduced to help poor pensioners, but is projected to pro-vide state financial support to 75% of all pensioners by 2050 as a result of the rapid growth of means-testing. The government's new Child Trust Funds or "baby bonds" have introduced the state into people's lives as soon as they are born, while the Sure Start programme has extended the state's influence during their early years.

Why has this occurred? In the words of Professor Anthony Giddens, a prominent theorist of New Labour, "Only a welfare system that benefits most of the population will generate a common morality of citizenship."

This pattern of state growth is no accident. Rather, it has been the result of a distinct ideological commitment within the Blair/Brown government, especially on the side of the Chancellor. In abandoning the language of state socialism, Gordon Brown's vision of the state has nevertheless been extremely broad. It is one in which, in effect, a new level of intervention has been added.

In the Brownian vision, the state does not merely carry on its traditional functions of taxation, policing and defence, or the post-1945 functions of the welfare state, or the commitment to active labour and industrial policies of earlier Labour governments. On the contrary it, and specifically Whitehall, has a direct relationship with all British citizens and residents. Almost all will contribute to taxation and a majority will receive some form of financial support, which will be rationed according to need; either by means testing, or via *ad hoc* transfers made at the discretion of the Chancellor, such as the Winter Fuel Payment and the Council Tax Rebate. In the name of efficiency, there will be a minimum of hierarchy or other intervening institutions between the Treasury and the home. The ethos of government will be one of continuous intervention and micro-management, in which specific groups will be targeted and economic incentives tweaked in order to redistribute resources or change behaviour—with huge complexity and fraud in the tax system as a result. Standing in the centre, mediating these transfers, and assessing merit or worth, will be central government; and in particular not merely the office, but the person, of the Chancellor of the Exchequer. The Gord Giveth, and the Gord taketh away.

This vision owes much to the Scottish Kirk, a church in which similar themes of absence of hierarchy, individual worth and salvation, all-inclusive community and a direct relationship with God are to be found. And there is a further important shared theme: a commitment to moralising. The central focus of a Kirk service is normally on preaching; on the transmission of Presbyterian principles ultimately based on the Westminster Confession of Faith of 1647. Similarly, the Brownian state is not merely a vehicle with the power to do good, and motivated by a political desire to do so. It is a channel for the transmission of certain values throughout society.

But we should not expect the state under Blair and Brown to have been shaped by a single vision. In fact there have been two other themes, both led latterly by the Prime Minister. One is that of *dirigisme* or central direction in the French style. Tony Blair came to power promising to lead a "Napoleonic" government, and in this regard he has succeeded. The role of the cabinet has been much diminished, and a new cadre of special advisers hired alongside career civil servants. The centre exercises much tighter control over departmental spending, over dealings with the press and "news management", and over appointments.

The final theme is a corporate one: the state as national corporation, with the Prime Minister as chief executive and the Chancellor as chief financial officer. Historically, the constitutional role of the Prime Minister was that of first among equals in the cabinet. Over the past thirty years this has morphed into a role as CEO, as both the principal commissioner of policy change and its main political implementer. We can see the influence of the corporate model in such things as "UK PLC"; the Prime Minister's "Delivery Unit", the central office charged with ensuring that No. 10's plans are achieved; the proliferation of public service "targets"; a heavy reliance on financing that does not appear directly on the national balance sheet, whose true cost is often unclear; a growing view among politicians of civil servants as economic agents or employees of the government, rather than as servants of the Crown; the vast extension of Prime Ministerial patronage; the relegation of government departments from being semi-autonomous entities towards a new status as divisions of the whole; the view of citizens as "clients" or "customers"; and the increasing informality and absence of procedure at the top of government. Some of these trends existed before 1997. Some existed before 1979. But all have been greatly accelerated under Labour.

The problem of productivity

Some of these developments are to be welcomed. But many will regard them with unease, whatever their own political affiliations. Those on the right may feel a natural instinct to rein back what they see as the fell hand of government. Those on the left, even if they regard the state as generally beneficent, may nonetheless feel concern at its impact on individual liberties.

The questions we want to ask are not ideological, however but practical. They assume rather than question the vital importance of having good public services in this country, of high quality and open to all. They are about means, not ends. Is this new statism working? Is it well-suited to the social and economic problems of the 21st century?

The clear evidence is that it is not. On the contrary, the inefficiency of the state is undermining our long-term productivity. Productivity is an abstract concept, which is notoriously subject to change and hard to measure. The term broadly refers to our ability to generate goods and services more efficiently over time: to get more output from a given input. It is thus a basic driver of a country's long-term prosperity.

The UK is often thought to be similar in its cultural and economic expectations to the US. But as regards productivity, the difference is marked. The US has gone through a productivity revolution over the past fifteen years, a step-change in its underlying ability to produce goods and services. And the trend in US productivity growth, having shifted up a notch in the 1990s, is now accelerating. The main reason lies in the interaction between two things: first, the traditional advantages the US offers to business such as flexible labour markets, relatively low taxation and low regulation; and secondly, the degree to which its companies have pushed the new telecoms and information technologies into their businesses, especially in manufacturing and retailing.

The UK has seen almost all the same technologies over this period, and in areas such as telecoms it has even been ahead of the US. Yet it has not seen a step-change in productivity. On the contrary, its performance has steadily weakened over the past ten years. Nor is UK productivity growth accelerating. Quite the opposite: it is growing more slowly than in the past, more slowly than in our main industrialised competitors in North America and the EU and in Japan, and far more slowly than in China and India. And UK productivity is specifically being pulled down by the performance of the public services. Notably, a joint report by the Treasury and Downing Street Strategy Unit found that public sector productivity fell by 10 per cent between 1997 and 2003.

This is all the more worrying because the Government has not been idle in its efforts to stop the decline. On the contrary, Gordon Brown famously remarked in 1997 that "the key to strong public services is long-term prosperity through higher productivity." Productivity, he rightly acknowledged, is "the fundamental yardstick of economic performance". True to this view, in every year since 1999 a section of the Chancellor's Budget Report has been devoted exclusively to the topic of boosting productivity, and Mr Brown has announced a vast array of measures designed to achieve this. In 1999 alone these included: increased capital allowances, the Research and Development Tax Credit, Enterprise Management Incentives, reforms to the Enterprise Investment Scheme, a Venture Capital Challenge, Individual Learning Accounts, a Small Business Service, and new tax incentives for corporate venturing. Every later year has witnessed a similar flow.

Many if not most of these initiatives have quietly fallen by the wayside, though some have had positive effects. Yet even where they have done so, it is all but impossible to imagine them making a material difference to national productivity. Take the R&D Tax Credit, for example: the Government's largest policy initiative aimed at improving innovation, running at a current cost of £700 million per year. This became effective after 2000. Business R&D spending stood then at 1.2% of GDP, and the Government gave a target of improving it to 1.7% by 2014. Since that time, overall business R&D spending has not grown more quickly as intended. In fact, it has not grown at all.

We can say with near-certainty, then, that the problem of weakening UK productivity is heavily concentrated within the public sector; and that repeated efforts by the Government have made little difference.

What of existing public services, though? What is the impact of slowing productivity on them? Take the NHS. Funding has doubled in cash terms since 1997. It will increase by a further third by 2008. Of course, some of this money has gone into improving services and health outcomes. But it has also meant that NHS costs have risen fast, by 4.2% in 2005-6 as opposed to less than 2% in the economy as a whole. NHS labour costs are set politically from the centre, and are not closely geared either to the economy as a whole or to local labour markets. So these rises are bound to cause continued deficits, as they are already starting to do. But NHS productivity growth has, even on the most favourable estimate, been just 1% p.a. since 1999.

The NHS is in an extraordinarily difficult position. It is a near-monopoly provider stagnating in a market of escalating service expectations, with which successive governments have continuously interfered, and to which the British public is deeply attached. In the longer term, however, what are the alternatives for the NHS in its present form? There are only two. Either it consumes more and more public spending, crowding out other important public priorities; or it grows its spending at the long term growth rate of the economy and does less with what spending it has. As costs rise outcomes must fall, in the face of both clinical standards and basic human expectations.

Even amid the present expenditure boom, we can already see this occurring. For example, renal dialysis is now not generally available on the NHS to those over 65. Given other priorities, the awful truth is that it is less expensive if they die. Women giving birth in NHS hospitals have less support from midwives than ten years ago. Costly new drugs with proven therapeutic effects are already being rationed or withheld. Patient preferences, such as the preference among many diabetics for inhaled over injected insulin, are being ignored. Premature babies, who could go on to live happy and worthwhile lives, have been described by one of the Royal Colleges of Medicine as "bed-blockers" impeding the treatment of other babies. Such is the pressure on resources. The NHS is already starting to look at "lifestyle" factors such as obesity and smoking in deciding whether a given treatment is available. These trends can only continue.

A similar pattern can be seen in pensions. The Turner Commission recently concluded that private pensions were in "serious and probably irreversible decline", while the pension system overall "is not fit for purpose ... and will deliver increasingly inadequate and unequal results". And we can see the pattern again in housing, and in education. The conclusion must be that it is less and less credible that the state alone can continue to fund and plan not merely the new public services of the future, but even our present public services as they stand.

Why, then, is public sector productivity in such a bad way? The reasons are not hard to find. The state has had nearly 800,000 new employees since 1997. Dozens of new quangoes, and an unnecessary new regional layer of government, have been created—and while the proliferation of new private sector organisations tends to create competition, the trend in the public sector is for new organisations to cross-refer to each other, with further paperwork and loss of productivity. An enormous number of new policy initiatives have been launched across all departments. Structural changes to the welfare state over the past fifteen years have created massive new complexity in the tax system, in benefits and in pensions. Paperwork has increased: Hansard reported in 2002 that schools had received 3,840 pages of instructions the previous year; the Child Poverty Action Group benefits handbook has relentlessly expanded; while the rulebook of the Financial Services Authority, which regulates the City, now stands at 8,500 pages. There have been well-publicised IT problems in HM Revenue and Customs; in JobCentre Plus; in the Child Support Agency; in the Department of Environment, Food and Rural Affairs; in the NHS over patient records; in the Foreign Office; in the pension credit system; in the courts; and in the administration of incapacity benefit.

The overall picture, in short, is not merely that the state itself is less efficient than it should be. It is increasingly hard to manage at all.

Baumol's cost disease

Now it might be argued that these problems are relatively short-term, stable and circumstantial: merely teething problems, after which everything will settle down, and efficiency and productivity will return. In fact, however, these problems are long term, almost certain to increase, and intrinsic to the nature of the public services.

To see why, we need to make a brief detour into the performing arts. In 1966 the economists William Baumol and William Bowen published a seminal article on productivity in the performing arts. The problem is this: imagine you are a member of a string quartet. Every year you and your colleagues need a pay-rise. But your productivity hardly increases. You can't drop a member and still play the Hoffmeister quartet with three people, and when you do play it, it will still last about as long as it did when Mozart wrote it in 1786. If you worked in a car factory, on the other hand, there would be no problem: productivity has risen hugely in the car industry as a result of technology, automation and supply chain management. This generates gains, part of which can be passed on to employees. Costs go up but output, normally, goes up faster.

This phenomenon is known among economists as "Baumol's cost disease". It arises generally in service industries, which tend to be hard to automate, hard to standardise, and reliant on the personal touch. If you have ever wondered why new car costs are falling while car repairs are more expensive than ever, then this is a large part of the answer.

Now of course our public services are just that: services. Hospitals, schools, and old-peoples' homes are precisely the kinds of places whose productivity it is hard to raise above their trend rates. Technology can make some difference, it's true; lectures can be webcast, x-rays can be emailed, day surgery can replace long periods in hospital. But the scope to increase productivity in services is much less than in manufacturing. Moreover, it is not always clear why you would want to automate services, as anyone who has ever called an automated telephone system will testify. Proper care and attention is what many of these services are about; it's what makes them valuable. Nurses cannot tend to patients, nor can teachers mark essays, much faster now than twenty years ago; or if they can, perhaps they should not.

Baumol's cost disease is no-one's fault; it's just an economic fact of life. But it raises the stakes of the present discussion in three ways. First, it makes clear why the problems identified here must be an inescapable and long-term part of the wider political debate. Secondly, it underlines the costs of present policy: the cost of the Government's inability to keep public sector productivity near its long-term trend rate; and the degree to which its recent policy of state growth without state reform has missed the opportunity to make structural changes while there was still money and time to do so. Finally, even once current inefficiencies in state delivery are addressed, Baumol's cost disease will put huge long-term upward pressure on tax revenues as a percentage of GDP. It makes it impossible to dodge the question of whether the state should continue to provide the services it does over the longer term.

Beyond the state

For these reasons, then, our present reliance on the state will prove unsustainable over time. In the words of WB Yeats, the centre cannot hold. We are over-wedded as a nation to the state, and to a single model of public service provision, and the effect is to impose a huge and growing burden of risk on all of us.

We need to think beyond the state. This idea may seem alarmist and irrelevant in the face of our current prosperity. To see why it is not, let us compare again the UK of today to that of the 1970s. The solution to the country's economic weakness at that time proved to be an extraordinarily brave and difficult set of supply-side economic reforms under the Thatcher government, which broadly succeeded and which form the bedrock of our current prosperity.

In the 1970s, however, our leading competitors were the US, Germany, France, and fast-developing Japan. All of these were democracies that took around 35%-40% of national output in taxes and spent it heavily on their public services. Capital was relatively immobile—far less mobile than in 1900, for example—and international travel was growing, but still not a mass market phenomenon.

Today, all this has changed. We live in the age of globalisation. Capital is extremely liquid and economic migration is growing rapidly. The UK faces huge competition; not least in the area of taxation, as low-tax economies entice more large and mid-sized corporations to set up shop within them. Our economic competitors are, as well as those listed above, the countries of Eastern Europe, China and India. These countries have different social models and different, and arguably lower, social expectations. And they are challenging us at precisely the time that the European social model is starting to fall apart.

Many of the effects of globalisation will be beneficial to the UK, as companies reduce costs and develop new markets for their products. For those reflecting on the future of the state, however, globalisation is likely to make the political choices still harder. Messrs Blair and Brown may wish to see themselves in the boardroom of UK PLC, but the irony is that their actions as managers have in many ways been directly contrary to best corporate practice. Therefore restricting and not enhancing British economic growth. They are the slaves of some defunct management consultant.

Of course, the global business environment is extremely diverse and pluralistic, one in which different models and strategies constantly arise, breed and die. But even so, best practice is rather stable across the largest companies. It includes pushing power and responsibility down to the lowest possible level; de-layering management; setting clear lines of accountability; agreeing firm budget constraints on spending; intelligent use of IT; cost control, often through outsourcing and moving operations offshore; and a strong focus on teamwork and staff morale.

The British Government has adopted some of these practices. But, in general, its departments are increasingly centralised, not localised; they are heavy, not light, in middle management; they still operate under rather soft budget constraints; they have little genuine transparency or accountability; they are highly inflexible in their strategy, working practices and ability to meet local needs; and they are constantly kept in the political cross-fire.

Some of this is hard to avoid, indeed desirable. Government departments are not corporations, and there is a need for them to be kept suitably accountable. But many of these problems have been created during the past ten years, and this highlights the need for deep and thoroughgoing reform. At some point the present very favourable macro-economic conditions will end, and we will face the unforgiving reality of an economic downturn, against competitors who are fitter and leaner than ourselves.

But there is also a moral argument to be made. Labour has accrued tremendous political capital by defining itself as the party of compassion and "social justice" against the supposedly uncaring Conservatives. Notably, Mrs Thatcher's remark that "there is no such thing as society" has been misinterpreted as reflecting a hardhearted indifference to the needs of the poor, the old and the sick.

Viewed in the round, however, Labour's own record on social justice—however we define it—is itself rather patchy. Take inequality, for example. On the standard economic measure, the heavy redistribution of income between 1997 and 2003 made no improvement to economic equality whatsoever. Indeed it got slightly worse over the period. But this in itself is cause for concern. If a serious and thoroughgoing attempt to redistribute income cannot make real overall gains during the longest period of British peacetime prosperity in recorded history, this in itself highlights the severity of the long-term challenge and the need for new thinking.

Meanwhile, whatever its positive achievements, we should note that the expansion of the state has also had clear effects in undermining social justice. It has resulted in an incredibly complex benefits system that the poor struggle to understand; a savings system that often deters saving; police forces that increasingly face inwards, not outwards to deprived local communities; "baby bonds" that pay twelve times as much money to well-off children as to poor ones; a housing system that is slanted towards smaller flats and less green space; schools that have more new buildings but less freedom to teach; a criminal justice system that offers less access to the victims of crime; and an NHS that is struggling to raise its performance in the knowledge that weakening productivity in fact means fewer operations, less treatment, more sickness and earlier death. Meanwhile, 3.8 million more people in Great Britain have been brought into the tax system, 2.7 million of them among the less well-off, and the poorest quintile of the population pays a higher percentage of its income in tax than the richest. Where is the social justice in all this?

In 1989, Gordon Brown wrote in his book *Where There is Greed*:

> *Quite simply, if Britain is to do even moderately well over what's left of the 20th century and on into the 21st, the determining fac-*

tor will be our competitiveness in a world of technology-driven
products, of custom-built goods and of precision items where the pre-
mium is not just on individual innovative and entrepreneurial flair
but also on the skills, adaptability and collective effort of us all.

This diagnosis somehow ignores the service economy, which has in fact
been the engine of British economic growth in the 1990s and 2000s.
But the focus on competitiveness, innovation and skills remains broadly
correct today. What is not correct, however, is the final inference:

And that will necessitate a greater role for organised and support-
ive interventions by the state.

On the contrary, what we are seeing today is the testing to destruction
of the idea of the state as a remedy for social failure. Key parts of British
society now need renewal, of a scale and energy last seen in the economy a generation ago. The question is from where, if anywhere, this
renewal can come.

2: It's the society, stupid

What improves the circumstances of the greater part can never be regarded as an inconveniency to the whole.' No society can surely be flourishing and happy, of which the far greater part of the members are poor and miserable.
Adam Smith, *The Wealth of Nations*

The times in our lives when we are able to look beyond money are those when we have enough of it. Retirement, perhaps, and childhood, if we were born lucky. What is true of people is also true of nations. Whenever Britain has enjoyed a period of sustained prosperity, its attention has shifted from economic issues to social and cultural affairs. Causes that may seem like luxuries when growth is slow and incomes are low suddenly become pressing when circumstances improve. In the 1880s, successive governments pursued social reform, to improve the squalor and misery of industrial urban life. In the 1950s, a "Butskellite" consensus emerged between a Labour party that had set up the welfare state, and a Conservative party that was happy to entrench and expand it.

Now, in the early years of the new century, a phase of relative plenty and stability is once again relieving us of the kitchen-table worries of jobs, prices and incomes. Ironically, it does so at precisely the time when the spending tap is running out and we may need to be on our economic mettle again.

For the present, however, we are more likely to be moved by inequality: of opportunity and outcome, at home and abroad. We are less troubled by economic ills than social ones such as crime and family breakdown, and by long-term environmental issues. Economic management, the most salient issue to voters in the 1970s and 1980s, has declined as an electoral issue. Elections are now won or lost on the battlefield of public services, with law and order also priorities.

Less perceptibly, there is a sense in which we are all, or are all supposed to be, bohemian now: the growth of healthy eating, gym membership, and the self-help industry are all signs of a society pursuing personal development in a wider sense than the purely monetary one. The conspicuous compassion of post-Diana Britain—the charity wristbands, the Fairtrade campaigns, the Live 8 concerts—speaks of a society that cares, or at least wants to be seen as caring.

Diana is a common and rather trite sociological point of reference. But the huge popular reaction to the murder of little James Bulger by two 11 year-old boys in 1993 now looks more and more like the moment Thatcherism ended. Not because the public accepted the idea promoted by the then Shadow Home Secretary, Tony Blair, that the failure of passers-by to ask why two boys were dragging a crying child through the streets of Liverpool was the product of a "walk on by" society somehow unleashed by the Tories. But rather because people were jolted into recognising that, while major questions of economic management had more or less been settled, there were still dark corners of British society and culture that remained untouched. There were neighbourhoods with no sense of community, and therefore no internal self-policing mechanism; and families with no parental authority, and therefore little means to share ideas and values. Only the most shameless partisan would blame inequality for the Bulger murder. But it was still true that pockets of social deprivation existed so extreme as to make some kind of lawlessness almost inevitable.

Of course, the desire for material improvement has not disappeared. But it now competes more with the desires for greater happiness, for better quality of life, and for membership of a safer and more decent society. No longer fearful of rampant inflation and confiscatory taxes, Britons now want a good local school as much as a bigger house. They worry as much about the time they can give to their children as about the things they can buy for them. They balance pride in their own position on the social ladder with awareness of the struggles of those below.

For the metropolitan middle classes in particular, social pathologies such as crack use, hoodies and "happy-slapping" are not merely unfortunate blights on distant estates, but genuine sources of concern and fear. How meaningful is it to be able to buy a three-storey house, if half the neighbourhood is a no-go area for your children, and what does it say about the position of the children who already live there?

The risk of consensus

Prosperity has not merely changed our political priorities. It has also affected our wider willingness to debate social concerns and the fundamental principles to be invoked in solving them. Yet this willingness has not been reflected in our answers, which have been unimaginative, statist and authoritarian: think of ASBOs, or CCTV, or identity cards. A nation once defined by its suspicion of the state has found itself looking ever more expectantly at government, and more often at Whitehall than at the town hall. We endlessly grumble at politicians and the decisions they make, but we rarely discuss in any deep or systematic way where their responsibilities as ministers end, and where our own responsibilities as citizens begin. We relate to government almost as spoilt teenagers relate to their parents: on the one hand, loudly cursing its interference; on the other, quietly counting on it.

Britain has been here before. From the inception of the welfare state in the 1940s to the breakdown of the Keynesian consensus in the 1970s, there was little or no principled debate in this country about the proper role of the state and its relationship with the individual. Of course, intellectuals and politicians argued over what would work and what could be afforded. But these were essentially technocratic discussions, which assumed in advance the desirability of state intervention to advance some imaginary "general will". Questions about the implications of an expanding state for individual freedom and for the vitality of civil society were rarely asked and rarely answered. In sharp contrast to the rich theoretical arguments of the interwar years, and of the period since the 1970s, both of which demolish the stereotype of Anglo-Saxon disdain for ideas, public and academic debate on key social issues during the 1950s and 1960s was curiously sterile and muted.

The consequence of this gap in thought and in public discussion was something rather more serious than a lean period for political philosophy. It allowed Britain to sleep-walk slowly into the agonisingly protracted and socially disruptive breakdown of the 1970s. Britain briefly became a society with an unargued and unsustainable consensus as to the necessity of state growth, and no willingness to debate the proposition. It therefore lacked either the means or the persistent interest to hold the Government to account on this most crucial of issues; or on its consequences, from nationalisation to industrial policy to trade union militancy. And so the corporatist assumptions that made all this possible, broadly accepted by governments of both parties during the post-war period, were never subjected to the over-arching philosophical scrutiny that would have led to their moderation, or perhaps abandonment.

There is an interesting parallel here to be drawn with the world of business. In the 1980s there was a huge wave of hostile takeovers in the US and the UK. The official story is that these were driven by a divergence between fundamental asset values and the lower prices at which shares could be bought in the market place. Predators borrowed cash, bought the shares, sold off the underlying assets and pocketed the net proceeds.

This was certainly true for some companies. But the real, broader story is more interesting. This is that many companies were not so much poorly managed as poorly owned. Their shareholders did not properly engage with them, did not hold them to account, and did not reward them sufficiently for performance: encouraging them to develop the best leaders and managers, supporting tough operating decisions, supplying capital needs, and requiring stringent cash management and satisfactory financial controls. It was this disengagement that permitted, indeed encouraged, the market for corporate control to operate via takeovers, takeovers that proved to be both industrially dislocating and financially expensive for many of those involved.

There can be steady change, or there can be delay and then abrupt correction. In a similar way, one might say that Britain in the 1950s and 1960s went through a period of being "poorly owned" by its citizens, who were above all happy at the end of war and distracted by new ideas, and that this complacency amid prosperity played a part in storing up later trouble. Only the most foolhardy optimist would rule out the possibility that we are near the end of such a cycle at the present time.

Flawed debate

Politically, then, these are times of broad consensus. This spells trouble to many in politics, academia and the media, who thrive on the conflict of ideas and fret that consensus means a cosy and complacent belief that all problems can be managed in the normal course of things.

Yet, as three consecutive election defeats testify, the reality remains that the right has failed to mount a genuine challenge to this consensus. It has disputed, but it has not made the argument. It has been unable to engage convincingly with our changed political priorities as a nation. Instead, the Conservative party has had to take cold comfort from Mr Blair's committed occupancy of the centre-right in British politics and Mr Brown's unwillingness to tamper with the structural economic reforms of the Thatcher years. Rather than tap its own intellectual history for a new strand of conservatism: a reinvigorated vision of society that could change the terms of the debate outright, the party has allowed itself to be presented with a false choice between betraying its own principles and defying public opinion: between either accepting the beneficence of an expanding public sector, or opposing social reform as such. This is the "Blair trap", sprung by the Prime Minister's remorseless focus on occupation of the centre ground.

So much is well understood. What may not yet be understood, however, is that the left has been caught in exactly the same dilemma. In equating social justice with redistribution and state spending on the public services, it has tacitly adopted a grossly inadequate conception of society itself. Even when big government has manifestly failed to relieve social ills, the left has tended to respond by calling for more government, rather than revising its views once more from first principles. In the most troubled parts of our country—such as the Glasgow housing estate where an 11 year old girl was recently found comatose from smoking heroin—the state is ubiquitous, providing the houses people live in, the schools they attend and what little income they receive. This dominance of the local economy and infrastructure, which has been in place for half a century, has coincided with the lives of residents in these areas becoming worse in many ways, not better. Yet the left still does not ask: when the state fails, what then? And even if it desired to ask this question, it is not clear that the intellectual space exists for it to do so, let alone to give an answer.

But "society" is not merely a set of sections or groups to be assessed and placated, of interests to be satisfied, and needs to be filled through rational direction from above. It is a sprawling and intangible network of trust and reciprocity without which even the most rudimentary interaction could not occur. In society, people relate to one another horizontally: they identify each other as equal members of the same civic whole, and do things for each other, at least partly, through mutual recognition, mutual respect and goodwill. People relate to the state vertically: they tend to defer to politicians and bureaucrats as those in charge, and obey them in part through fear of sanction. But society is organic, not official: it cannot be established by law or fiat, but evolves through time and practice. Above all, it is delicate. An invasive state disrupts the voluntary bonds between people, linking them upwards to the government rather than sideways to each other.

Compassionate conservatism

This, then, is the political context. As we shall see, compassionate conservatism seeks to change the terms of this debate, by presenting a new and positive vision of society which emphasises these "sideways" linkages between people.

But in order to do so, it must confront two initial challenges. Call them the "old left" and the "new left" challenges. The old left challenge is well-known and widely held: the idea of compassionate conservatism is an oxymoron, a contradiction in terms. On this view, conservatism is about unleashing people's basest instincts: a greed for material possessions and a fear of losing social and economic advantage. It uses markets to set people against one another, and these markets do not cure social injustice and poverty but create and perpetuate them. Conservatism is thus ideologically opposed to compassion, whatever "compassion" amounts to. In the face of this, only the state has the power and the social opportunity to stand up for people against the market.

The new left challenge is more subtle: we've been here before. This is just political posturing. There is a centre ground in British politics, which Thatcher redefined and Blair occupied. Compassionate conservatism is just a vague cliché, another move in the power game, an attempt to revive a dying brand and identify a line of intellectual succession from Thatcher to Blair to Cameron which is rhetorically predisposed to favour the Tories. It is not an intellectually distinctive set of ideas. Nothing genuine or new is happening here.

The new left challenge can go further: it can claim that compassionate conservatism is just communitarian thinking in disguise. Many centre-left intellectuals, if not necessarily centre-left politicians, have long acknowledged that markets may be beneficent and big government not problematic. Indeed, American academics such as Robert Putnam and Amitai Etzioni have explored the crowding-out effects that state action can have on civil society. This provides further reason to think compassionate conservatism can have nothing new to say. And if it could, the challenge continues, if there were indeed a need to rein in the state so as to advance social justice, then this is a task that we should only entrust to those who have credibility to manage both the state and social justice; that is, the left.

These, then, are the challenges. Both are misconceived. But to see why, we need to look more closely at conservatism itself.

3: Compassion vs. conservatism?

I am a nineteenth century Liberal. So is Mrs Thatcher. That's what this government is all about.

John Nott, Secretary of State for Defence

As a body of political thought, conservatism is all but impossible to define. The career of Benjamin Disraeli illustrates the point perfectly. The young Disraeli opposed social reform, for the sound conservative reasons that it eroded property rights and local independence while increasing taxation and regulation. Thus he voted against cheap bread in 1846, against the Public Health Act of 1848, against the Mining Act of 1850, and against the General Board of Health Act in 1854. He opposed the Privy Council's idea in 1839 to give the Committee in Council on Education £30,000 to spend on educating the English poor, so much did he fear the intrusiveness of state inspection of schools.

The older Disraeli, on the other hand, led social reform as Prime Minister for the sound conservative reasons that it relieved poverty, squalor and hardship, and promoted social cohesion, or "One Nation" as we have come to call it. He won the 1874 general election by pitching the Tories as the party of real reform against a Liberal cabinet which he derided as "a range of exhausted volcanoes". He spent the next two years passing eleven major acts of social reform across a number of areas, including trade union rights, factory conditions, public health, education and housing. During this legislative flood the condition of the people, rather than the interests of the landed, became the central preoccupation of the Tory party.

Just the kind of unscrupulous U-turn to be expected of conservatives in general, it might be argued, and of Disraeli in particular. Haven't the Tories always been political magpies, picking and choosing between ideas to suit the moment, ruthlessly appropriating their opponents' most popular themes, discarding hitherto fervent beliefs once they cease to be expedient?

It is easy to deride Tory statecraft as the subjugation of abstract principle to the practical goal of winning and maintaining power. It may be lauded as flexibility or condemned as cynicism, but it must be recognised as indispensable to the popularity of conservatism as a political creed. It was not by accident that the Conservative party spent two-thirds of the 20th century in government. Disraeli himself cited the enfranchisement of the industrial working class as a strategic imperative to support social reform. Had he not been heeded, the Tories might have gone the way of the Liberals: electorally diminished by a principled refusal to buy off the assertive new voters.

However, this is only half the picture. A further look would show that this tension between principles is intrinsic to conservatism itself. Not only that, it is a crucial reason why conservatism has been so extraordinarily successful over the years as a political movement. The Tories' habitual switching between different strands of ideas is not merely the product of electoral calculation. Rather, it reflects genuine philosophical tensions within conservatism as a body of thought. The Conservatives have been a "broad church" in electoral appeal precisely because they have been a broad church in ideas.

Thus, to take only a few examples, conservatives have called for greater social cohesion, but also for individual freedom. For free trade, but also for protectionism. For imperialism, but also for isolationism. For central standards and efficiency in government, but also for local independence from Whitehall. For the relief of poverty, but also for lower taxes. For stronger links to Europe, and for weaker ones.

Two traditions

Historically, in Great Britain these principles have clustered around two rival traditions: a liberal or libertarian conservatism concerned with free markets, localism and private property, and a paternalist conservatism that has prioritised community and social stability.

Of these, the latter has been more prominent over the past two centuries. Indeed Conservatives were legislating trade union rights a generation before the Labour party was founded, and establishing public health projects before Aneurin Bevan was born. Disraeli's last ministry represents a 19th Century high watermark of Tory paternalism, while the Macmillan government, whose "middle way" entrenched and expanded the welfare state forty years before Blair's "Third Way", represented such a mark for the 20th. By contrast Thatcherism, as the quotation that opens this chapter attests, was something of a throwback to Gladstonian liberalism, with its rolling back of the state, its moral fervour and its emphasis on individual freedom.

Often, however, there has been stalemate between these traditions. From the arguments over social reform in the mid 19th century, to the defections over free trade in the early-20th century, to the "wet" resistance to the New Right in the 1970s, to the current debates about tax cuts and academic selection, British conservatism has had contradictory instincts on public policy and the role of the state: one urging greater scope for individual initiative, the other more reconciled to large and active government. That both these contrasting principles can legitimately claim to belong to the conservative intellectual tradition is precisely what makes the dilemma so agonising.

It is also a peculiarly British problem, as centre-right parties in most Western democracies have chosen one way or the other between the two traditions. The mainstream conservative parties of Europe, such as Germany's Christian Democratic Union and France's Gaullist party, are essentially comfortable with a paternalist view of the state as an agent of social change and the embodiment of the nation. Europe's decade-long affliction with low growth and high unemployment has pushed these parties in a reformist direction. But the most far-reaching proposals for economic liberalisation still come from smaller liberal parties hoping to find their way into a coalition government. The spectacle of Jacques Chirac, a notionally centre-right President, defending the European social model from such tentative reforms as the EU Services Directive captures the degree to which paternalism runs deep within the marrow of continental conservatives.

By contrast, to simplify still more grossly, centre-right parties in the Anglo-Saxon world, namely the US Republicans and the Australian

Liberals, have traditionally espoused an essentially liberal brand of conservatism. They have emphasised self-reliance and voluntarism over benign big government, most recently of course in America with a strongly Christian backdrop. With the important exception of Ronald Reagan's presidency, the Grand Old Party's recent flirtation with fiscal profligacy represents an aberration from the mainstream of American conservative thought. It was not until the Eisenhower Republicanism of the 1950s that the American right reconciled itself to Franklin Roosevelt's New Deal reforms, and it has taken 35 years for it to accept the permanence of Great Society programmes such as Medicare. The neo-liberal triumphs of the Clinton years such as welfare reform, the balanced budget resolution and the absolute cut in federal payroll were all conservative ideas forced by a Republican Congress on a reluctant Democrat President. Only on national defence, and on hot-button cultural issues such as abortion, have American conservatives consistently envisaged a role for a large and active state.

Another British curiosity is that the two traditions of conservative thought seem to switch sides when the debate shifts from economics and public services to the legal and moral issues of nationhood, criminal justice and foreign policy. Here, it has been those on the liberal or libertarian side who have appreciated the utility of the state as a "bully pulpit" from which to cultivate patriotism against what is seen as a dangerously rootless post-modernity; who tend towards a more aggressive posture on law and order; and who are more willing to employ the armed forces in the pursuit of British interests abroad.

Conversely, it has been those on the paternalist side who have been sceptical of both the principle and possibility of a state-led civic nationalism, who are mistrustful of state expansionism and centralisation in criminal justice, and who have preferred cautious, stability-maximising realism in foreign policy. This again serves to illuminate the complexity and heterogeneity of conservative thought.

Context and instinct

As in the political arena, so in the intellectual. Conservatives do no less thinking than liberals or socialists. The difference is that they have never settled on a conclusion. Conservatism is in effect a cluster of ideas competing with each other for market share, of which a prominent one is paternalism. It may be periodically out-competed by its libertarian rival, but it never goes out of business. Libertarianism enjoys peak periods, but never a monopoly. Even Mrs Thatcher among Conservative politicians was sufficiently mindful of paternalist imperatives to make no serious attempt to cut back public spending on health or education.

Which of the two traditions holds sway in any given situation depends on nothing more high-minded than the circumstances that obtain at the time. Context is crucial. The practical conditions of the here and now guide conservatives as surely as pre-written doctrines guide socialists and utilitarian liberals. A political conservative must determine the requirements of a particular situation, and reflect on which of his or her principles are to be deployed and how. This may require a shift from one principle to another over time, or the simultaneous application of different principles to different situations. Such shifts may be disdained as hypocrisy, and of course sometimes they may actually be hypocritical. But politics is not logic. Absolute consistency in the application of abstract principle to practical politics is rarely possible and never wise. The British electorate, with its preference for common sense over grand theory, usually rewards this insight at elections, even as it abuses it between them.

What ultimately distinguishes conservatism from its rival creeds, therefore, is not so much the views it holds, though some of these are unique to conservatism, as the way it holds them. Socialism and liberalism are, at root, theories and ideologies: fundamental interpretations of the nature of history and of "the good", from which policy programmes are supposedly inferred. Conservatism is no such thing. It is instinctive, not theoretical; a disposition, not a doctrine; realistic and sceptical, not grandiose or utopian; accepting of the imperfectability of man, not restless to overcome it; and anxious to improve the lot of the many not by referring to some plan, but by working with the grain of what Kant called "the crooked timber of humanity". It is precisely its reluctance to accord sacred status to any abstract idea that allows conservatism to incorporate so many of them. It is precisely its refusal to regard change as a good in itself that makes it uniquely qualified to manage change most prudently.

So much is true, but it is not enough. Any political perspective with a claim to government must explain how it will address contemporary problems, not merely insist that it will do so with a cool head and an even temper. It must offer a principled critique of things as they are; explain what principles it stands for, and which tradition it stands within; and set out a distinctive and politically useful understanding of society that can help us shape a solution. To this we now turn.

Not views it's the way their held.

4: Rethinking our assumptions

The men who create power make an indispensable contribution to the Nation's greatness, but the men who question power make a contribution just as indispensable, especially when that questioning is disinterested, for they determine whether we use power or power uses us.

John F. Kennedy

To adapt a celebrated motion on the monarchy of 1780 in the House of Commons, the power of the state has grown, is growing, and ought to be diminished. We have seen how our political debate has conspired to shape the apparent available options against conservatism as a political force. And we have seen the remarkable flexibility and range of conservatism as a body of ideas.

If any alternative exists to the present statist consensus, it must be here. But what is that alternative? Where can we find a coherent, positive, humane and long-term view of how our society can be improved, independently of the state?

Compassionate conservatism has such a vision within it. But before we can see that vision, we need to dig down, briefly, to philosophical bedrock: to Thomas Hobbes, and to Michael Oakeshott. At this point on our journey into the interior, the argument briefly gets a bit more theoretical.

Our basic theory of the state derives largely from Hobbes. Hobbes was born in 1588, his birth reputedly brought on by his mother's alarm at news of the Spanish Armada, and he died in 1679 at the age of 91. He thus spent his youth in the era of Shakespeare, Jonson and Donne; his middle age during the constitutional crises of the 1630s, from which he fled to Paris in 1640 just in time to escape the English Civil War; and his old age in the midst of a scientific revolution that, inspired by the insights of Galileo, Descartes and Newton, continues to this day.

Hobbes was employed throughout most of his adult life as tutor to the Cavendish family, that of the Earls (and later Dukes) of Devonshire; and while in Paris he also acted as tutor to Charles, Prince of Wales. Yet despite, or rather because of, this background, he did not shrink from addressing the basic philosophical question: on what legitimate basis does British government exercise its powers? Or to put it another way: by what right does the state exist?

In his book *Leviathan*, published in 1651, Hobbes argued that human government owed its existence to a contract between all members of society, by which they voluntarily traded autonomy for security. In the absence of government people lived in a state of nature, a "war of all against all", in which all were constantly at risk and constantly afraid of violent death; a state in which people's lives were, in his famous phrase, "solitary, poor, nasty, brutish and short". The social contract is simply a rational response to this fear. Individuals cede some freedoms on a once-and-for-all basis to a single sovereign authority which, by guaranteeing civil order and external boundaries, gives them the space and the legal and physical protection to associate freely with each other.

It is this act of empowerment that makes society possible. The sovereign authority may in principle be a single person, a group of persons, or indeed the people themselves. It may be a monarchy, an oligarchy or a democracy. But it and it alone is the source of legitimate power, and its legitimacy derives from being freely given by all. The sovereign can properly pass legislation because we, the people, have authorised it to do so; and according to Hobbes we are under a moral obligation, not merely a legal obligation, to obey its laws for the same reason.

Hobbes's genius lies in providing an account of sovereignty that locates its authority in the voluntary choices of individuals, not in an act of God or in some dubious and ill-defined collective will. His account is so familiar as to be the common currency of practical politics even today. Of course, few if any nowadays would follow Hobbes in his more extreme views: in seeing the sovereign as absolutely powerful, or the people as giving up all their freedoms to the sovereign through the social contract. But nevertheless it seems that many people, including those who have neither read Hobbes nor even know his name, possess an instinctively Hobbesian conception of political authority, grounding it in rational self-protection, rather than in any divine bequest.

Yet its very familiarity has blinded us to its consequences. For what *is* this contract? Not a description of any historical event, but an idealisation of a legal relationship between the individual and the state. The formal beauty of this idealisation is that it makes no assumptions as to human motivation or interests, beyond assuming that all are solely motivated by the fear of violent death. It is thus the intellectual precursor of the economic models of today. In economic theory, at least until recently, human psychology is normally regarded as irrelevant. The issue is (supposedly) not what motivates an individual to act as he or she does, but what assumptions can explain and predict most simply and accurately how people act in the aggregate. People are thus treated as though they are purely self-interested seekers of profit or some other form of "utility"; individual atoms cut off from each other, who react positively to opportunities for gain and negatively to the possibility of loss.

Hobbes, in effect, does something similar. For him, humankind is not innately bad, but people naturally desire freedom for themselves and control over others; they are, in his words, continually in competition for honour and dignity. It is these desires that, unfettered, render the state of nature so abhorrent. But it is specifically the fear of violent death that motivates the social contract. This is a minimal basis for the existence of the state.

In defining the state, therefore, and in order to define it, Hobbes has defined the individual as well: the two are point and counterpoint to each other, the two basic elements from which his politics is derived. But if we reverse the image, so to speak, and ask not what is included but what is left out, what do we find?

What we find is that Hobbes makes three crucial omissions, which still set the terms for current arguments about state and society today. First, he deliberately ignores, as we have seen, the astonishing richness and diversity of human emotions, aspirations, interests and goals.

Secondly, in his extreme individualism, in seeking to rule out any such thing as "the people", or the "common will" as such, over and above actual individuals themselves, he deliberately ignores all intermediate institutions between the individual and the state. The family, the church, the club or guild—and today, the union, the company or the team—are secondary entities, created by individuals once they have achieved the protections of the social contract. Civil laws are, in his words, but chains from the lips of the sovereign to men's ears—with nothing in between.

Finally, Hobbes builds in a moral presumption in favour of the state and against the individual. After all, the social contract is freely entered into by us; indeed the sovereign state just *is* us, to the extent that it represents our pooled and delegated authority. According to him, we cannot demur or grumble, therefore, when our authorised sovereign acts in ways of which we do not approve, except when it threatens our survival. We have freely empowered it, and if it acts contrary to our interests, then tough luck. There can in general be no conscientious objection or civil disobedience in Hobbes's state.

Like the social contract itself, these omissions cast a very long intellectual shadow. Indeed they still structure present debates over the nature of the state and the political alternatives available to us. We shall come back to them in due course. For now, the key point is that the social contract à la Hobbes is designed to explain the rightful existence, authority and legitimacy of the state, but at root it says nothing whatever about society, or the relationship between state and society. We may know that the sovereign authority is authorised to pass laws, and that individuals are obliged, and can be properly compelled, to obey them. We may know that the social contract is what allows society as such to come into existence at all. But we know nothing more. We have an outline, but none of the fine detail or colour.

But unless we understand the two notions of state and society better, we have no chance of seeing what is at stake here: what, if anything, we are giving up by allowing the state to grow continuously, or what an alternative vision of our society might be.

The essential tension

For this, we need Michael Oakeshott. Oakeshott's was the pattern of an outwardly uneventful academic life. He was born in 1901, and died in 1990. He studied at Cambridge, and then taught there, at Oxford and at the London School of Economics. During his long lifetime, he published two books of essays and two monographs, each of the latter in its own way a masterpiece—and each sufficiently rigorous and unfashionable in viewpoint as to fall, like Hume's *Treatise*, dead-born from the press. He is little known and less read today. He lacked any formal academic qualification in philosophy. But he has rightly been called the greatest British political philosopher since Edmund Burke.

Oakeshott, in effect, draws a distinction between two kinds of society: civil society and enterprise society. A civil society is an association of citizens, individuals who are formally equal in their rights before the law. As citizens, they have something in common with each other. But this is not a common goal, or purpose, or plan. Rather, it is just that they recognise that they are all bound, one no more and no less than any other, by a system of laws, and that these laws are passed by a single civil authority.

An enterprise society is very different. It is one in which the whole of society itself is organised as a communal enterprise or undertaking in its own right. In this case, individuals are not viewed as citizens, endowed with certain basic rights and protections. Rather, they are seen as contributors to a common project, who come together to achieve a recognised goal or goals. These goals may be economic, such as greater national prosperity or industrial productivity. But they need not be. They may be cultural, ethnic or religious goals, such as cultural unity, ethnic purity or religious orthodoxy. An enterprise society thus has nothing as such to do with business or "enterprise" in that sense. On the contrary, its overarching purpose may be entirely different.

As one might expect, these different types of society operate according to different rules. In a civil society, the rules will generally be procedural, not substantive; they will set frameworks within which people can live, not targets for them to achieve. They will be universal not specific, applying to all and not identifying certain subgroups of citizens for gain or penalty. And they will say what all citizens must do as a matter of obedience to the law, not in virtue of a commitment to engineer certain social outcomes. In a civil society, the function of government is not to do anything as such, it is just to govern. The state has no goals or projects of its own, over and above those of the individuals or groups being governed. Instead, its role is to devise, promulgate and enforce laws by which people may go about their private business in an orderly and secure way.

In an enterprise society, on the other hand, the function of government is precisely to achieve certain social objectives. It can never be content merely to govern. It is, as it were, ambitious. The laws it creates will tend to set specific goals, to assume the state's right to manage people, to treat people as a means to achieve the state's own priorities. Government in an enterprise society can never rest easy, for nothing is ever as good as it could be, and so there will always appear to be scope for state intervention to improve it. If poverty or economic underperformance or crime exists, it is but a short step for the state to take upon itself the task of improving the situation.

We can readily see both conceptions at work in British history: the notion of civil society in such things as Magna Carta, legal due process and voting rules; and that of enterprise society in Great Britain PLC, the No. 10 Downing Street "Delivery Unit", five year plans, public service targets, and the national bid to host the Olympic Games in London.

Oakeshott's two conceptions of society are idealised, of course. Neither is, nor ever could be, exemplified in its pure form, and so every actual society has elements or aspects of each. The two are, however, distinct, indeed formally exclusive of each other: philosophically, one is organised under the category of procedure, the other under that of purpose. In short, they are rivals, struggling over the soul of a given society, forever pulling it in the directions of self-restraint or ambition as each gains or loses the upper hand, in an essential tension.

So much for the theory. Why does this distinction matter? The first thing is to note that the 20th Century was the century of the enterprise society. State provision of goods and services in the name of common social goals grew rapidly in every major industrialised country around the world. Of course, those in authority have never been indifferent to people's economic or social well-being, on pain of unrest, loss of office or revolution. But for the state itself to be used as economic engine, safety net or service provider has been a modern, and specifically a 20th Century, innovation.

We have already seen how this occurred in the UK. But it bears remembering that the most extreme forms of tyranny in the last century arose from what is, intellectually, the same source. Both communism and fascism have a common root in their desire to organise all of society's resources to achieve a set of "social" goals determined by the state. In communist Russia, officially at least, these goals included the achievement of a "classless society" and the "dictatorship of the proletariat". The chosen means included the expropriation of private property; the nationalisation of agricultural and industrial production; huge programmes of forced industrialisation and collectivisation; the central administration of exports, imports, prices and incomes; and state control over banks and other financial institutions.

In contrast, Nazi Germany preserved much of the form and some of the substance of private property, free markets and democratic institutions. But it too was a heavily enterprise society. Its goals were economic recovery, the achievement of national racial and cultural purity, and ultimately of course the military occupation and control of Europe. Nationalisation was only used selectively. Instead, companies were organised into cartels under administrative boards, allied to banks; the unions were broken and wage controls imposed; there was a huge programme of public works; and an enormous mobilisation and expansion of the armed forces. The story of how Nazi Germany sought to achieve its other goals is too well-known and too awful to need re-telling here.

To many people, each of these very extreme examples of tyranny is a one-off, a unique social phenomenon unlike any other. To find a pattern between them, let alone to link them to processes and events currently at work in modern western democracies, may seem at best poor reasoning, and at worst simply offensive.

Yet they do serve to bring out a more general principle: that the growth of the enterprise society invariably tends to abridge our freedom before the law. Recall that the enterprise view is one that judges people, not as citizens, but by their contribution to some overarching corporate goal. In such a society, the interests of citizens are always subordinate to the overall project, which is invariably determined by the sovereign power, by the state itself. The best citizen is, thus, not a citizen at all, but a star worker, like the famous Russian miner Stakhanov; or a star entrepreneur, or parent, or saver, or taxpayer. Formal equality is thus replaced by a social metric assessing people by their contributions to the corporate whole; and, often, by a strand of public moralising that seeks to justify these assessments.

Fascism is thus the worst case of the enterprise society in action; the case in which all private interests are subordinated to the designated goals of the society itself. We can see this in Mussolini's infamous slogan "Tutto nello Stato, niente al di fuori dello Stato, nulla contra lo Stato" ("everything in the State, nothing outside the State, nothing against the State"). Or take a perhaps still more notorious example, Hitler's "ein Volk, ein Reich, ein Führer" ("one people, one regime, one leader"). This was not merely a call for Germans to associate themselves with a national project incarnated in the leader's own person. It was also a tacit invitation to ignore intermediate institutions or protective laws in so doing.

The idea of a connected society

Oakeshott brilliantly illuminates the relation between state and society: the essential tension between the claims of a civil and an enterprise society, and by implication the costs and benefits of Britain's steady transformation into a more purely enterprise society.

Yet there is a missing category in Oakeshott, which echoes what is missing in Hobbes. Like his predecessor, and for similar reasons, Oakeshott has merely given us a minimal specification. A civil society is based on procedure, a framework of laws between sovereign and citizen, but it is nothing more. An enterprise society is project-based, society conceived as an organised purposeful whole, but it is nothing more.

Everything else must be filled in. Each must be given an ecosystem: each must be populated with living, loving and dying human beings who come together in groups or institutions of every imaginable kind.

The omission becomes more telling if we notice that Oakeshott's fundamental categories of procedure and purpose are insufficient to describe some of these institutions. For what kind of association is a family? Or a football supporters' club? Or a company? Of course each obeys certain procedures, and each can have a purpose: bearing and bringing up children, cheering the team on, making profits. But anyone who thought of these institutions solely in such terms would only partly understand them. They would be missing a crucial feature, which helps to explain the centrality of these institutions in our culture. This is that in very different ways they are based in and constituted by human affection.

Readers of *Fever Pitch* will need no reminding of this. Nick Hornby's book vividly describes the emotions of the fanatical football supporter: the hero-worship, the dedication required to attend every match, the hatred of competing teams. Yet what sustains the supporter through the seasons, year in, year out? Not some top-down incentive plan; not the rules of the supporter's club; and not even the success of the team, as Newcastle United fans can testify! Surely it is the tribal feeling of belonging, of being inside the circle and part of the group.

If this is right, then we need to recognise a new category, a new kind of association, one based on affection rather than procedure or purpose. In the spirit of Oakeshott, we can call this missing category that of "connected" or philic association, after the Greek word *philia*, a word whose various meanings includes "friendship", "tie", "affection", and "regard". And with it in mind, we can restore what Hobbes has left out: a focus on human lives, and what allows them to flourish; a place between the individual and the state for all those intermediate "sideways" institutions which link us all together and give fulfilment to our lives; a counterbalancing moral presumption in favour of the individual; and a recognition that what motivates human beings need not merely be a matter of the stick and the carrot, complying with rules or achieving some collective goal, but of culture, identity and belonging.

So far so good. But it is not enough simply to recognise the possibility of a connected society, or even to describe certain institutions in
terms of their linkages, of the human connections that inspire them, or
of their place within the social web. We need to specify what a society
would be like that was organised horizontally, not vertically, so as to place
these intermediate institutions at its heart. This is the topic of the next
chapter.

5: Connection and identity

We form our institutions; and they form us.
Attributed to Sir Winston Churchill

*You can't handle the truth! Son, we live in a world that has walls.
And those walls have to be guarded by men with guns. I have a
greater responsibility than you can possibly fathom... You don't
want the truth. Because deep down, in places you don't talk about
at parties, you want me on that wall... I have neither the time nor
the inclination to explain myself to a man who rises and sleeps
under the blanket of the very freedom I provide, then questions the
manner in which I provide it.*
Col. Nathan R. Jessep, C/O US Naval Base, Guantanamo Bay,
A Few Good Men

At this point the reader may reasonably be feeling rather sceptical.
Where is all this going? Isn't a "connected society" just the kind of
debased verbiage which desperate politicos tend to reach for when they
have run out of ideas?

No. It would be a mistake to think of "connected society" as a term
of current political debate, to be deployed for tactical purposes against
the language of the "Third Way", "progressive universalism" and other
such mumbo-jumbo. Rather, in order to move the present discussion
forward, we need to keep "connected society" to its given meaning: a
society understood in terms of affection or personal tie.

As such, the idea embodies three insights. The first is that man is a
social animal. People are not merely sterile economic agents, but living,
breathing beings who find self-expression and identity in relation to
each other. The second is that, in so doing, people create institutions, of
an extraordinary range and diversity, and that these institutions them-

selves help to shape both the people who belong to them and society more widely. The third is that some of these institutions themselves stand between the individual and the state, acting among other things as buffers, conduits, outlets, and guarantors of stability.

This may seem pretty obvious—but the task of an explanation is often to rediscover or restate in other terms what we already know. Furthermore, this line of thought has quite radical policy implications, as we shall see. But these policies will be built on sand if we cannot spell out in a fairly punctilious way what a connected society amounts to and why it is valuable.

Start, then, with the basic idea of a society. At root, this derives from Roman law. In a society, the individuals are associates, or *socii* in Latin, who collectively belong and recognise each other as belonging, a recognition that creates a degree of mutual respect and obligation between them. These associates are equal and free, and the bond each owes to another derives its value from being freely given.

A society is thus in this basic sense an association free of class, hierarchy or any other inherited structure or institution that might constrain the freedom of individuals. And for the same reason, a society is and must be free from overwhelming concentrations of power. Power must be diffused; it must be shared and counterbalanced for a society to exist at all. The rule of law is both a prerequisite to and the specific creation of such power-sharing: institutions such as private property, or *habeas corpus*, or the independence of the judiciary naturally arise to protect existing freedoms and interests, and to permit new ones to develop. These institutions then serve as protectors of freedom in their turn.

A connected society goes one step further than this, however. It does not merely recognise the importance of institutions in the narrower, legal sense, such as those mentioned above: constitutional institutions whose role is to promote good order, restrain excessive power, and protect the basic freedoms of the citizen. It also recognises how institutions, conceived far more broadly, give shape and meaning to human lives. It takes the idea of mutual recognition that is implicit in the idea of society, and sees in it the aspect of personal regard, personal tie and personal affection that was missing, or perhaps assumed, in Hobbes and Oakeshott.

Edmund Burke is sometimes taken to be the father of this thought, in saying that "to be attached to the subdivision, to love the little platoon we belong to in society, is… the first link in the series by which we proceed towards a love to our country, and to mankind." But we should not restrict ourselves to the little platoons. The regiment and the brigade are no less important, so to speak. And we should not even at this stage exclude institutions that have no physical presence at all. So we are talking not merely about a particular local church, or rugby club or branch of the Women's Institute; but also about the market, the nation state and the city; and, more abstractly still, about the family, marriage, and the rule of law.

These institutions are not created and sustained merely by physical or emotional affection, of course. They each have a point and purpose of their own. But even at their most distant and discreet, they retain some tie to us, some claim on our personal loyalty. That tie may be deep or shallow, long- or short-lived, near or far; it may be the surge of patriotism even the mildest of us feels when someone insults our country; it may be our automatic respect for a local doctor or vicar whom we have never even met; or it may be the joy of discovering that a remote Indian village has someone with a radio tuned into the Test match.

Yet equally, the idea of a connected society acknowledges that our feelings and affections are always somewhere present. It is they that underwrite our loyalty and investment in these institutions. And as Aristotle identified, and as the Romans first made into a principle of statecraft, the most natural, the most particular and the most universal of these feelings are those of friendship.

We are a long way from politics now. But already we can see in outline a restated critique of the growth of the state. Recall that the very possibility of society rests on the diffusion of power. In a connected society, the sovereign state is one institution, albeit a privileged one, among many. As citizens, we may owe it our moral allegiance, as Hobbes believed; but as associates we also owe allegiance to each other and to the many different institutions that define us. The state is uniquely endowed with the power to coerce individuals according to law against their will. But precisely for this reason, it is under continuing obligations. First, to be restrained in its own actions, recognising its intrinsic limitations, and balancing its own remedies with respect for existing arrangements and organisations; and secondly, to enfranchise and support those very institutions in our constitution that inhibit its power and force it into dialogue.

The centrality of institutions

We can see our institutions, then, as the crucial missing third part of the story so far. Instead of the opposition of the individual and the state to be found in much political theory, we have a three-way relation, between individuals, institutions and the state. It is this missing aspect of connection that transforms a society from a centralised, we-they, economic pushmi-pullyu into a living, flourishing organism.

But institutions are not just the objects of our loyalty and affection, and the relationships that help define us. They are also, in Burke's further thought, the repositories of much human wisdom and knowledge. Unless newly created, in order to exist at all they have fought their way against competitors, learnt from setbacks and profited from advantage. In short they have been formed by experience. They thus embody the collective experience of previous generations, and this experience can and frequently does outstrip the wisdom of those who would reform them. A conservative, it has been said, is someone who recognises that institutions are wiser than individuals. But from the present viewpoint it is not clear that this is a distinct political stance at all. On the contrary, it is simply irrational to ignore the wisdom of institutions. The political question is what weight, under given circumstances, this should bear in the creation of policy.

This is true even for institutions that have no physical presence at all. A financial market, for example, may simply be a matter of ones and zeros on computer screens. Yet, as Adam Smith recognised, a market is not a memoryless place where pure economic agents come to transact.

It is a cultural entity, situated within a rich context of human practices, traditions and expectations as to such things as pricing, weights and measures, quality of goods or services, delivery, returns and future behaviour. And it is governed by conventions and rules no less powerful for being inexplicit. Markets too, then, possess their own wisdom, disaggregated though they may be.

Of course, this is not to say that all tradition is good; that what exists must exist; or that our institutions never require further justification. But it reminds us that change is not reform, and that reform must go with the grain of institutions if it is to have a positive effect.

The history of British government is littered with attempts at reform that have ignored existing institutions and so undermined them; and, correspondingly, with late rediscoveries of the wisdom of some forgotten tradition. Take the case of friendly societies. Between 1800 and the beginning of the Second World War, there was a huge advance in voluntary provision for sickness and old age by means of these working class mutual-aid societies. By 1938 over 20 million working people were registered members. Even an early 19th Century friendly society might provide benefits for sickness, unemployment and disability, as well as loans and a widow's pension. More services, including pensions, were added over time. It was run by the members and for the members on a one-member one-vote basis, so that costs were low and dishonest claims kept to a minimum. It was sustained by, and contributed to, a spirit of self-reliance and mutual support, which discouraged reliance on charity and on state provision.

The state first regulated friendly societies in an act of 1793. Over the following century, legislation further defined the rights and responsibilities of those involved. It was only with the National Insurance Act of 1911, however, that the state inserted itself into the collection of contributions. It compelled all wage-earners between 16 and 70 to join a health benefit scheme, to which the state and employers also contributed. The scheme was, however, still administered by "approved" friendly societies and members were encouraged to make top-up contributions in their own right. When cuts in public expenditure were required, however, in 1922, 1925 and 1933, the Government did not hesitate to reduce the state subsidy to friendly societies, many of which ran into difficulties during the recession of the 1930s. They were ultimately relegated to the margins altogether when the administration of these benefits was nationalised in a series of acts after 1945. There was little reason for them to be effectively eliminated through crowding-out by the state, however, and similar voluntary institutions did not suffer this fate in much of Europe.

Fast forward to today, however, and what do we see? The UK's company pension schemes, which were once the envy of Europe, now have total deficits estimated at £100-150 billion. They have been undermined by the unexpected withdrawal of tax relief in 1997 by Gordon Brown; but also by an earlier decision under the Thatcher government to tax the "overfunding" of schemes by their parent companies, which would have provided some buffer against present-day problems. Thus the wheel turns.

Conversation and identity

So far we have argued that human beings live in and through institutions. These institutions can be the objects of our loyalty and affection, they can mediate our relations with each other, and they can be the repositories of our inherited experience. We now need to ask, finally, how they interact with each other, how they can come together, and what effects this may have on our collective identity.

When we examine a particular society under the headings of civility or enterprise, we can see the state as sovereign authority in traditional categories, whether as passive enabler or as active, ambitious agent. In a connected society, however, the emphasis is not on the state at all but on culture and identity, on how people think of themselves, and why. This line of thought applies to all human societies, in principle; all may be seen in terms of connection, just as they can be seen in terms of civility or enterprise. But to see its political relevance today, we need to focus on British society, and on the well-springs of our own identity: on such things as our language and literature, our school history, our contribution to the rule of law, our experience of empire and its aftermath, and our traditions of teamwork, decency, irony, dissent and wit.

In so doing, we can think of the thread of cultural exchange as that of a conversation or dialogue. Different institutions, from different traditions, each have their own distinctive "voices": those of science, business, religion, the law, education, or the arts, for example. In a conversation each voice has its own character, yet each must speak in common terms to others if it is to be understood, to move, to persuade, or to command. How they develop, how they interact with each other, and how they are heard by different people, will determine the character of the conversation as a whole. Similarly, the character of a society will derive from the way in which its own cultural conversation develops, and is encouraged to develop.

The conversational metaphor is a rich one. In the first place, any conversation demands a context of mutual respect and order, in short of civility. This is a basic rule of conduct between citizens dealing with each other under the rule of law. In any conversation all voices have their place, and though they may be ignored once speaking, none is to be forbidden in advance from speaking at all. All are, in effect, regarded as autonomous and individual. Secondly, a vibrant conversation is one whose voices are diverse, mature, self-confident and independent: in short the voices of citizens, able to examine authority, to question it, and to hold it to account. Thirdly, conversation reminds us of the different possible roles of the media: as a conveyor of ideas that in principle aspires to be neutral between them; as a critic of established power; and as a voice advocating its own ideas in the attempt to wield power for itself. As the internet and new communications technologies continue to expand the range of conversation, our sensitivity to these different roles can only increase.

It is a distinctively European achievement to have first developed and brought together the fundamental institutions—the nation state, the rights of individuals as citizens to speak and associate freely, the marketplace, the political forum—through which our cultural conversation takes place, and from which it continues to spread out into the world. And it is this insistence on the acknowledgement of civil authority expressed through the rule of law that specifically differentiates the

European tradition from, for example, classical Islamic traditions, in which law and religion do not merely run alongside and reinforce one other, but are regarded as identical.

The idea of conversation also brings out what is most distinctive in the constitutional settlement in the USA. The genius of the American founders, and above all of James Madison, was to engineer a constitution that deliberately constrained and fragmented the power of government between state and federal levels; between executive, legislature and judiciary; and between House of Representatives and Senate. Each was thereby placed as a check and balance to another; and so all were forced into continuing conversation with each other, as to the issues of the day, and as to the proper scope and limits of the various parts of government itself.

Finally, the metaphor of conversation underlines the wider critique offered here. The present government is characterised by a default instinct to extend the powers of the state over the lives of its citizens. In conversational terms, one might think of the state as the domineering bore at the table, whose loudness overwhelms the talk of others. But a better parallel would be that of the patriarch in whose unspeaking presence others feel robbed of air and automatically fall silent. Similarly, the extension of the state, whatever its apparent short-term attractions, tends to undermine the voices, the energy and the creativity of its citizens. If it is hard to see this now, that may partly be because we have lost sight of how rich and fulfilled all human life has the potential to be.

The strength of diversity

The present emphasis on diversity and conversation does not merely spring from the conviction that these are valuable in their own right or as a means of social enrichment. We can think of them as crucial sources of social intelligence.

There is now a huge literature on the theory of "wise crowds": the phenomenon whereby diverse groups make better judgements, or solve problems better than experts. To be "wise", a group must satisfy four conditions: its members must be diverse, independent (each person exercising his or her own view, and not deferring to others), and decentralised (so people can specialise and draw on specific or local knowledge). Finally, there must be some means to aggregate or gather their private judgements or choices together into a collective decision. When these conditions are met, the results can be astounding. Compared to experts, crowds are generally better at estimating things (such as the weight of a rendered and dressed ox, in a 1906 experiment of Francis Galton); quicker at accurately assessing outcomes (such as the reason why the Challenger space shuttle blew up); better at estimating the outcomes of sporting events; and better at picking stocks and shares. And specifically, it turns out that groups consisting of experts are regularly less good than groups that also include non-experts under testable laboratory conditions.

It is perhaps no accident that the idea of a connected society that we have identified emphasises precisely the things that make crowds wise. Its whole focus is on promoting diversity, independent-mindedness and decentralisation, and much of the point of its insistence on markets and conversation is to enable these important aggregators of human opinion to function effectively. By the same token, however, other viewpoints seem to destroy social wisdom. Paternalism of any stamp encourages deference, and so "groupthink", the herd instinct whereby crowds can often act irrationally. The present statism is worse still. It undermines diversity, reduces independence and increases centralisation. A better recipe for foolishness in a society would be hard to imagine.

More generally, the theory of wise crowds adds force to the critique of enterprise society, or one organised from above as a single purposive entity. It suggests that such societies have an inherent tendency to lack wisdom and hence social and economic success, compared to more diverse and pluralistic models. There is a paradox here: that organising society as an enterprise in fact kills enterprise. On the contrary, it is only insofar as societies are genuinely enterprising and empowering of individual energy and creativity that they can succeed.

Nevertheless, there is an obvious objection to this line of thought. Now this talk of conversation is all very well, it runs. But it's really just soft-centred jaw-jaw, isn't it? Just donnish after-dinner pass-the-port self-indulgence, the kind of worthy but irrelevant theorising we have come to expect from those who lack the power to take tough decisions in the real world. In the real world, as the quotation at the start of this chapter from the film *A Few Good Men* reminds us, not everyone is civilised. There's not much point meeting bombs, crime and hatred with fine words.

In fact, however, this argument is a weak one. There is little reason why a nation committed to the values of a connected society should be anything less than utterly resolute in defending them. Quite the contrary: the history of warfare suggests that it is often those very values that have inspired the greatest achievements on the battlefield. The Athenian statesman Pericles made this point in his funeral oration of 431 BC, in contrasting the openness and democratic values of Athens with the narrow military authoritarianism of its bitter rival, Sparta:

> *Our system of government does not copy the institutions of our neighbours. It is more the case of our being a model to others... Our constitution is called a democracy because power is in the hands not of a minority but of the whole people... There is a great difference between us and our opponents in our attitude towards military security... [and] certain advantages, I think, in our way of meeting danger voluntarily, with an easy mind, instead of with a laborious training, with natural rather than with state-induced courage.*

Similarly, in combating terrorism, the first battlefield is over the hearts and minds of a nation's own citizens and residents. Of those who fret that a concern for free institutions and cultural conversation mean weakness we can simply ask: what are *you* seeking to defend?

The British experience

It is of course true that different people will have different views of British identity. But this is as it should be. The point is not to trade intuitions about what is or is not authentically British, but to note the consequences of the focus which a connected society naturally places on culture and identity.

The first is simply to understand, however unfashionable it may be to do so, that there is something extraordinary and distinctive about Great Britain and its island story. This is a matter not of any God-given right to rule but of our language, of our institutions, and of the example we can set to ourselves and others. *Il y a une certaine idée de la Grande Bretagne*, to paraphrase General de Gaulle. This is not cause for complacency, nor for self-depreciation or condescension. It is simply how we are, a way in which others see us, and something for us to live up to if we can.

We are accustomed to think of democracy as the supreme expression of human self-governance. But as Hobbes reminds us, the most fundamental such achievement is in fact the rule of law, since without the rule of law no government can take place at all. And historically, this country enjoyed the rule of law, to greater or lesser degree, for around nine hundred years before the creation of a full democracy in the modern sense. It is the fundamental institution in which we as a nation are invested, and by which we have been formed.

Again following Hobbes, we are apt to think of law as requiring a sovereign to enforce it. But this need not be so. A people may be so bound by its own collective sense of identity as to feel constitutively obliged to obey its own laws, even where no genuine enforcement exists. Obeying the law can simply be part of its identity. Arguably, this is now true of the Jewish diaspora. It may also be true of Britain: that respect for the law, and indeed respect for other traditional values, is partly constitutive of what it is to be British. Any derogation from these values in foreign or domestic policy would then be, to that extent at least, an erasing of what it is to be us: a kind of suicide.

If this is true, it would help to explain the peculiarly anguished nature of the recent debate over the invasion of Iraq, for example. But it would also have a direct impact on British relations with Islam more generally. For many Muslims are, it seems, bound in a similar way by their adherence to Sharia law, wherever in the world they may be. The stage is thus set for possible conflict between the British sovereign demand for obedience to civil authority, and the constitutive requirement on traditional Muslims, including of course those in Britain, to obey the Sharia. The point is not to be alarmist; it is simply to note the basic similarity of the commitment on each side.

Finally, there is a more specific source for concern. It is well known that many of the powers of Parliament have been ceded over time to the European Union. Nevertheless it remains true that in England and Wales (matters are arguably rather different in Scotland) a democratically elected government can – in principle at least and provided it is sufficiently persistent – make or amend any law by a simple parliamentary majority in the House of Commons. This flexibility is an important aspect of the British constitution. Yet, from the present standpoint, it also creates a deep problem. As the state grows, as executive power increases and constitutional safeguards decline, as the UK becomes ever more an enterprise society, it is inevitable that the status of the rule of law itself must increasingly come under threat. With no formally entrenched basic law, and in the face of weakening respect by government for constitutional conventions that have historically had the force of law, the question is simply this: on what long-term basis is the rule of law itself to be upheld?

The answer can only be on what we understand about ourselves, and our traditions and values: on our sense of identity as a nation. If this is correct, the kind of intelligent reflection on British identity and British institutions that we have called for in these pages is not optional. Indeed, it is both essential in its own right, and as a prerequisite to much other policy-making.

Compassionate conservatism again

Back to politics. We have now described the idea of a connected society more fully. Our claim is that it is this conception of society that should be the central focus of British policy-making. The challenge for all of us is to develop public policies that recognise, protect and enhance our connected society, and that enrich the cultural conversation within it.

The idea of a connected society implies certain limitations. It discourages the concentration of power in any particular organisation or person, public or private. It is self-aware and modest in its expectations for government. It understands the need for economic growth, but it does not regard economic growth as the only source of well-being. It does not favour any particular section or group within society, except for those in poverty: whether through lack of cash, experience or opportunity.

However, the idea of a connected society is far from modest in its optimism and ambitions, for individuals themselves and for the multifarious ways in which they grow and develop. It recognises the social bond that we each owe to one another, and the role of institutions in creating and strengthening that bond. Here again, the idea of conversation can guide us to the right way forward: to trust people; to invest in their virtues and not their faults; to welcome aspiration, energy, innovation and plurality; and to support and extend the institutions that carry on our distinct traditions as a nation.

We can understand recent discussions of "compassionate conservatism", mentioned in the Introduction, as an attempt to express this line of thought within British politics. But in order to do so we have to separate this phrase from its connection with the doctrine of the same name espoused by George W. Bush before and during his first term as US President. This was a campaign slogan originally adopted in 1999 to emphasise to the public that Bush was a moderate Republican, while subtly flagging a sensitivity to the concerns of religious evangelicals. After his election, it mutated into a policy of delivering federal welfare programmes through churches and other faith-based organisations. It was abandoned when its chief sponsor within the White House, Professor John DiIulio, quit in 2001.

In fact, however, Bush's compassionate conservatism has virtually nothing to do with the ideas we are discussing, for three reasons. First, it suffered from the twin drawbacks of being neither compassionate nor conservative. It was hardly compassionate: indeed DiIulio fell foul of his colleagues in the White House by insisting that money be directed to black and Latino churches, thus alienating white Evangelicals. And it was not conservative, as was shown by the extension of federal influence into local schools through the *No Child Left Behind Act* of 2002. Secondly, Bush's compassionate conservatism was a moralising doctrine, which assumed that society's basic moral standards were in decline and set the federal government the task of improving them. Thirdly, as a slogan, "compassionate conservatism" lacked a deeper theoretical justification that could be used as a basis for long-term policymaking. It quickly came to seem merely an electoral expedient, not a genuine contribution to a wider political and cultural debate.

The compassionate conservatism that we are discussing is quite different. It is anchored in an argument from first principles about the nature of society. It is not a moralising strand of ideas, and does not in general regard the moral character of British society as fit subject for legislation. Indeed it explicitly repudiates such a view in its critique of "enterprise society", something that also sets compassionate conservatism apart from many communitarian views. It does not lack a moral sense, but it locates moral responsibility primarily at the level of the individual, not at that of the state. And consistent with this, its idea of compassion is one of fellow-feeling, not of pity: one of identification, concern and sympathy with others, not of condescension to them. At root, this is the same insight as that behind the connected society.

British politicians who espouse compassionate conservatism have recently been criticised in the media for having little of substance to offer the policy debate. The present analysis suggests, however, that this is mistaken. In saying "we're all in this together" and that "there is such a thing as society; it's just not the same thing as the state", they are in fact articulating intuitions that are both intellectually coherent and well-founded in conservative principles.

Equally, however, compassionate conservatism belongs to neither the paternalist nor the individualist traditions of conservatism. It is closest to another tradition, the distinct and long-ignored "Old Whig" tradition, with its roots in Adam Smith and Edmund Burke, and its modern flourishing in Oakeshott and Friedrich Hayek.

It is not paternalist, because it is realistic about the capacity of the state to improve our lives; and because it does not assume a relation of subservience between "we" and "they", between governed and governor. On the contrary, it is egalitarian. It sees our elected politicians as the Ancient Greeks saw them: as citizens first and foremost, in whom a temporary, limited and qualified trust has been placed to exercise public power on our behalf. And in keeping with its emphasis on conversation, this trust in turn implies mutual consideration and respect, and a pushing down of power and accountability away from the centre and towards the people.

Yet compassionate conservatism does not regard individuals as mere economic agents, or as composing groups or segments of society which must be successively wooed and bought off with favours from government. It is not the desiccated economic atomism of the "Chicago school" of economists, in which individuals are understood as isolated agents, cut off from others. It insists not merely that we are all in this together, but that *all of* all of us is. A political viewpoint that ignores human dignity or energy or creativity in the name of a sterile economism, impoverishes itself to that degree.

No. Compassionate conservatives will be closer to Hayek when he said that the whole nature and character of individuals is determined by their existence in society. Markets are then seen for what they are: not as ends in themselves, but as both as the greatest means yet devised to generate wealth and prosperity, and as having the inherent capacity to promote freedom and so to challenge bureaucratic authority.

The old and new left challenges revisited

Chapter 2 described two challenges, from the old left and the new left wing, to the very idea of compassionate conservatism. Either it is a contradiction in terms, or it's an empty slogan. We can now see that both are wrong: the first, because it rests on a caricature of economic liberalism that the compassionate conservative has already rejected; the second because it underestimates the fertility of the intellectual tradition we have identified.

This tradition is a distinct and substantive one, unnoticed in political debate for decades, and not a mere slogan. It is recognisably conservative in its scepticism about the power of government, its respect for institutions, its pluralism, and in the scope it accords for individual energy to flourish. And it is compassionate both in the root sense of acknowledging our fellow-feeling with each other, and in drawing the circle of our moral concern around those with whom we are, and have been and will be, interdependent.

It remains to be seen how this vision can be translated into policy. To this we turn in the final chapter.

6: From identity to policy

Any man's death diminishes me, because I am involved in mankind. And therefore never send to know for whom the bell tolls. It tolls for thee.
John Donne

I repeat … that all power is a trust; that we are accountable for its exercise; that from the people, and for the people all power springs, and all must exist.
Benjamin Disraeli, *Vivian Gray*, 1826

And so to policy. We need to ask "So what?" Where's the beef in compassionate conservatism? How can we take these ideas and make something of them relevant to policy?

At this stage in most policy papers there would now follow a long list of things that government should supposedly do. But the whole point about compassionate conservatism is that it is at root a view about what we, the people, can do for ourselves: how we can directly improve the society, the environment, the relationships and institutions in which we find ourselves. Nevertheless, the desire to create and sustain a connected society has profound implications for government at three levels: of principles, of the policy context, and of the creation of policy itself.

Three principles

In a connected society, as we have seen, the emphasis is on individual freedom and autonomy, on diversity and pluralism, on the institutions that link people together, and on an awareness of common culture and traditions. Compassionate conservatives thus perceive, in the French thinker de Tocqueville's words, that "the more [the state] stands in the place of associations, the more will individuals, losing the notion of combining together, require its assistance. These are cause and effect that unceasingly create each other." For them, however, reducing the power of the state is not only desirable in principle, as the precondition to a better society. It is also the means to secure better public services, greater social justice, and greater freedom and economic prosperity. The debate, then, is not about whether these latter things are important, but about how to achieve them.

This suggests three broad principles of political action. The first is one of freedom. It recognises that many interventions by the state are of necessity coercive, and others may be desirable. But it insists that individuals, as citizens, should enjoy a default presumption for freedom and against state interference in their lives. The counterpart of this freedom is that individuals should take a greater degree of personal responsibility for their lives. After all, if the state is the means we use to pay for our health, welfare and education, then we can expect it to take an interest in how we are doing.

The second principle is one of decentralisation. It pushes political power and responsibility further down to individual citizens, saying that political decisions should where possible be taken close to the people they affect. In other words, those whom we have empowered to act must do so in plain sight, ideally from within a given community. That community will vary. Some decisions must be taken nationally, in defence for example. Some must be taken internationally, such as those governing trade and market access. But many more could and should be pushed down to the local level.

The third principle is one of accountability. It allows citizens to exercise their political will effectively by insisting that those in political power should be clearly accountable to the citizenry for their actions. This is to ensure better performance on pain of removal, and to maintain the legitimacy not merely of our public elected offices but of a political system that places elected office at its core.

These principles underline the extent to which compassionate conservatism is about limiting state power, and preserving and extending our democracy. As we have argued above, however, democracy is not the only British political value. It presupposes the rule of law, and so it presupposes that our constitutional arrangements are working well. In Great Britain this means above all the sovereignty of the Queen in Parliament.

Our constitution has evolved so as to embed the power of the executive within that of the legislature, and to balance what results with the independent power of the judiciary. The power of the judiciary is not merely part of our constitution, however. It is specifically and democratically ratified by Parliament. If the judiciary acts to restrain the power of the executive in some way, it is always open to Parliament, in which the political party of the executive will normally have a majority, to overturn the relevant law or to recuse itself from the relevant international convention. Indeed, it is theoretically open to Parliament to repeal all or part of the Act of Settlement 1701, on which the independence of the judiciary formally rests.

British democracy thus deliberately constrains itself in order to function more effectively. It sets limits to accountability, and so to the zeal of even the most ardent reforming democrat. From the present perspective, however, this suggests that the principles above have a deeper grounding in our inherited legal traditions and way of life. It is, indeed, intrinsic to the idea of compassionate conservatism to seek to understand, and to trust, the wisdom of these inherited institutions; to resist attacks on them; and to help them to function more effectively.

Standards, information and transparency

It is in policy, however, that compassionate conservatism must show that it can make a difference. It needs to offer a rich and distinctive basis from which existing policies can be judged, and new policies developed. Or else it will be consigned to irrelevance on pain of being too broad or too bland.

The first thing to note is that it suggests a radical rethinking of the approach taken by government to policy itself, in three areas: standards, information and transparency. In recent years, a wide gulf has opened up between our understanding of best practice in policymaking, and what actually occurs in and around government. Take the public statements through which government sets out options for change known as "green papers". These are rarely thoughtful explorations of the costs and benefits, or the principles and working assumptions, of different policy options including the option of doing nothing. More often they are thinly disguised marketing documents designed to advance an agenda that has already been broadly decided by government. The Government's recent green paper on incapacity benefit is a case in point.

The effect of this is to patronise the public, to undermine the credibility of government, and to set the terms for death by a thousand leaks as the hidden political motivation becomes clear. A recent exception has been the first Turner Report on pensions, published in 2004, which is a balanced and thoughtful analysis that has genuinely moved forward the public understanding of these extremely complex issues. But in so doing it has simply highlighted the deficiency elsewhere, and the need to spread good practice more widely.

Compassionate conservatives will want to open this whole process up. They will want to insist, for example, that government publish a set of standards for its own policy development and then adhere to those standards; that it be more explicit as to the expected timing of major legislation, with longer lead times; that it encourages a wider range of independent organisations to submit parallel policy proposals of their own; and that the best such proposals be explicitly considered by government in the framing of legislation.

It is evident that as a nation we cannot discuss what political actions to take in the absence of well-framed and properly costed options. But the growing importance of having independent sources of information available to all has also been rightly recognised in recent years. Compassionate conservatives will want to take this process too a step further. For example, there should be far more transparency over the exact costs of the Private Finance Initiative. And there is a strong case for creating a summary set of national accounts that briefly and simply show not merely public expenditure but the value of tax relief. This information is available, but it needs to be consolidated so that the full picture, both of government spending and tax foregone, is clear.

Needed: an audit of government

So far we have looked at the principles and background to policy making. What we now want to suggest is that compassionate conservatism also offers a new way to approach the process of policy creation itself.

As we noted in Chapter 1, in recent decades the state has consumed a broadly steady percentage of GDP in taxes, at between 35% and 40% of the total. But this trend disguises significant change in the composition of state spending. Items such as defence, state subsidies to industry and debt interest payments have fallen significantly, while spending on education, health and social services has risen. As we saw, the economics of Baumol's cost disease implies that, given the state's heavy orientation towards services, upward pressure on its spending is likely to intensify. Successive governments have been able to keep state spending on a more or less even keel, at least until recently, by substituting expenditure on services for expenditure on other items such as debt interest.

The importance of this line of thought is threefold. First, it reminds us that what the state spends our money on has always been a fit topic of debate. There is nothing new, and nothing inappropriate, in questioning the limits of the state. Indeed as we saw in Chapter 2, problems come when debate ceases. Secondly, it underlines the point that substitution can only go so far; and that when it ceases state spending will be under inexorable pressure to rise. And thirdly, it forces us to ask what the limits of social cohesion will be: will Britain allow government spending to drift upwards towards the 50%-60% now characteristic of the Nordic countries? And if it will not, how must the state be reshaped, and with what priorities?

What we need is a principled and long-term approach to this issue: a framework within which Britain as a whole can conduct a fundamental reappraisal of the proper role of government. This will start from the insight that there are in fact only a limited number of ways in which government can be effective. It can spend directly, it can regulate, it can privatise or nationalise, it can centralise or decentralise one of its own parts, it can license other organisations, or it can revenue-share with them, among other things. But this makes it possible to conduct an audit of the major government functions, asking in each case what its purpose and role is at present, what that purpose should be and how best, if at all, should be carried out in future.

It is inevitable, and right, that such an audit will force us to reconsider the limits of personal and local responsibility. Should individuals bear personal responsibility if they are ill as a result of their own unhealthy lifestyles? Should families bear more responsibility for old age care? Should a given community bear more responsibility for law and order, for education or welfare? And to what degree should the costs of these choices be imposed on others?

It will also be crucial to recognise the importance of risk in such an audit. Britain has a single model of the state, broadly speaking, and a uniform and top-down process of policymaking. The result is, as we have argued, that this country almost certainly has a huge long term exposure to unnecessary or unwanted risk.

This risk is not merely that of unexpected catastrophe or emergencies. It is the ordinary exposure we as individuals run every day because the state is not doing its job, or not doing it well enough: the risk of crime, financial loss, or disease. More widely, it lies in how we treat the environment, in our consumption of energy, and in transportation, education, benefits, social services, and health. In effect, the state is like a gigantic hedge fund, running a vast array of open positions in different financial markets, but with little assessment of risk vs. return, a weak regulator, and no debate as to other ways to invest.

One or two areas apart, there is little evidence to suggest that the British government has made any systematic attempt to measure or manage risk. Indeed its growing corporatism and authoritarianism are increasing the problem. For the present, the right approach is to include risk assessment in our audit of government from the outset. This would mean looking at different scenarios for each function: asking, for example, how a greatly decentralised NHS would cope with different levels of demand, whether its performance would be better or worse than at present, and in what areas.

This will hardly be easy. But the theoretical capacity to measure and assess risk has improved hugely in the past decade and such scenario modelling is common in business and finance. It is not a panacea but a normal tool of good management. It will almost certainly be painful in its effects, forcing Britain to acknowledge the long-term damage caused by its recent unreflective statism. But it would be a hugely innovative and important development in public administration. And it would be the crucial precursor to a thoroughgoing and long-term attempt to remodel the state so as to boost its productivity.

One might think that this kind of risk-based audit had little to do with compassionate conservatism as such. But in fact it springs directly from such a viewpoint: one that recognises the fundamental importance of good public services and seeks to improve them; that is sceptical of state monopolies, and celebrates independence and diversity; that genuinely looks to individuals to take responsibility for their actions; and that enfranchises our institutions to help fill the civic gap in our society. For these very reasons this viewpoint cannot be socialist, or paternalist, or merely economically liberal. Only compassionate conservatism will do.

Some policy implications
Imagine, then, that such an audit of government has been conducted. What are the kinds of policies we should expect, bearing in mind our earlier principles of freedom, decentralisation and accountability, and the image of a connected society?

- We might expect *a large-scale programme of state decentralisation*: pushing more power and responsibility back to local councils and town halls, cutting back regional government, deregulating key markets such as housing, and introducing greater competition into the benefits system and the NHS, for example.
- We might expect *much more empowerment of institutions*: such as long-term plans and transition funding for universities that wish

to become independent and offer needs-blind admission; locally elected police chiefs and opposition to the mergers of police forces; deregulation of the not-for-profit sector; and far more freedom and less bureaucracy for primary and secondary schools.

- We might expect a *greater emphasis on sharing British culture*: for example, through a voluntary programme of national public service aimed at old as well as young, through support for sport in and out of schools, and through policies that move away from the present multiculturalism that divides different ethnic and religious groups, and towards a greater civic awareness.

- We might expect *a celebration of individual freedom*: and so implacable opposition to ID cards, to DNA collection from the innocent, to a national identity register, and to the recent curtailment of freedom of speech; a drastic simplification of the tax system; and a drive to renew our rather seedy present political culture.

Even this short list would constitute a huge domestic policy programme. But compassionate conservatism also has implications for foreign policy. As we have seen, its emphasis is on culture and identity; on existing institutions and relationships; and on the distinctiveness of British culture and the Anglophone sphere. The Churchillian vision of a post-imperial Britain simultaneously playing a role in its "three circles" of Europe, America and the Commonwealth is truer to British culture, and more likely to maximise British influence, than a wholesale commitment to any one sphere.

This implies an assertive, confident nation state that is neither Eurofederalist nor purely Atlanticist. It implies a broad scepticism as to the removal of powers from Parliament to the EU, and a preference for international alliances over permanent structures. It implies support for other democratic nations, but also for non-governmental organisations abroad: the "little platoons" working to promote pluralism, diversity and the rule of law in other countries. Finally, it implies a self-conscious re-commitment to Britain's traditional civilising mission around the world. Indeed, the increasing globalisation of the media gives Britain a huge opportunity to reinforce—through language, through education, and through its distinctive institutions—its status as an oasis of civility, democracy, culture and conversation.

Trust and security

We said at the outset of this book that Britain faces two great problems in the 21st Century: a problem of trust and a problem of security. How should we strengthen our society? How should we protect it?

Our argument has been, in effect, that these can only be addressed by a more thoughtful debate as to the nature of British society, and of the British state. Only when we have a clear and settled vision of these can we take the political steps necessary to improve society. Only then will we know what it is we are protecting, and why.

Compassionate conservatism offers such a vision, from first principles through to policy outcomes. It is a vision that requires further thought, further development, further conversation, to be realised as policy—and this is a task for all of us. Turning it into reality will not be at all easy. To win big, we must be willing to risk failure. The kind of thoroughgoing decentralisation described above will bring with it huge political pressure, for diversity inevitably means different outcomes for different people. The benefits will be huge: greater energy, greater innovation, a more productive economy, and a more connected, engaged and safe society. The challenge will be to achieve a smooth transition, and this will demand courage, wisdom and maturity from all sides.

Acknowledgements

This is not a political, philosophical, economic or historical book as such. It is a hybrid, a work of political explanation whose main ideas have been several years in gestation. It tries to pull together ideas from different fields of thought into an argument from first principles through to a distinct political viewpoint, and then to show the relevance of that viewpoint to Great Britain today. Only in one or two places, and in the presentation of some of these ideas, is it original.

The book thus owes a huge amount to the work of others, as the end-notes testify. Among more recent influences, we would especially like to acknowledge David Willetts's *Civic Conservatism*, Charles Moore's inaugural speech as Chairman of Policy Exchange, and the writings of Lee Auspitz, Oliver Letwin, John Micklethwait and Adrian Wooldridge, Ferdinand Mount, Roger Scruton and Andrew Sullivan.

This book has also been much enhanced by the comments and ideas of independent experts, friends and colleagues. These include Kate Auspitz, Tom Bingham, Elizabeth Bingham, Nicholas Boles, Chris Cook, Greg Clark, Catherine Gibbs, Rupert Harrison, Alan Hodson, Rachel Kelly, Danny Kruger, Tim de Lisle, Bob Monks, Tim Montgomerie, Torquil Norman, James O'Shaughnessy, Peter Phillips, Henry Raine, Matt Ridley, Felicity Rubinstein, Andrew Sullivan, Martin Taylor, Romesh Vaitilingam and several academic readers who have preferred to remain anonymous. Needless to say, none is responsible for errors in what remains.

The authors would like to thank their colleagues at Policy Exchange, and especially Nicholas Boles and James O'Shaughnessy, who have provided such a stimulating and fun environment in which to work. Special thanks go from Jesse to Kate Bingham and to Sam, Nell and Noah Norman.

Endnotes

A note on terminology: in the text we deliberately use some shortcuts for reasons of simplicity or readability. "Great Britain" and "the UK" are treated interchangeably, except where the difference is relevant; and we generally ignore the contrast between Whig and Tory strands in conservatism, and use "Tories" as a synonym for "Conservatives". But we distinguish between "Conservatives" with a big "C", who are politically affiliated to that party; and "conservatives" who may in principle belong to any political party, or to none.

Introduction

Freedland: "Enough of this love-in: Bush was a compassionate conservative too", *Guardian*, 7.12.05

Toynbee: "Those who want to shrink the state forget who pays the bills", *Guardian*, 13.1.06

Wolf: "'Cameronism' is empty at the centre", *Financial Times*, 20.1.06

Stephens: "Murdoch's Muddle over Cameron", *Financial Times*, 23.1.06

Heffer: "The 'shock and awe' of Labour-lite Tories", *Daily Telegraph*, 7.1.06

Steyn: "Ideas win elections: glamour doesn't", *Daily Telegraph*, 10.1.06

Chapter 1: The state we're really in

UK economic prosperity: *Budget Report*, HM Treasury 2005

Drug use: European Monitoring Centre for Drugs and Drug Addiction, *Annual Report* 2005

Binge drinking: Institute of Alcohol Studies *"Binge Drinking" Fact Sheet*, 2006

Teenage births: *Innocenti Report Card*, UNICEF Innocenti Centre, July 2001

Children in workless households: *Monitoring Poverty and Social Exclusion in the UK 2005*, Joseph Rowntree Foundation

Voting patterns: *Power to the People*, the POWER Inquiry, February 2006

Life expectancy in Scotland: In-house research based on NHS data, *The Scotsman*, 2 January 2006

Thatcher government and the state: Simon Jenkins, *Accountable to None*, Hamish Hamilton 1995

Tax burden: *Pre-Budget Report* 1997

State employment: Fraser Nelson, *Spectator* 25.2.06

Anthony Giddens, *The Third Way*, pp. 108

Changing nature of government and its corruptions: see P. Oborne and S. Walters, *Alastair Campbell*, Aurum Press 2004

Gordon Brown on productivity: Pre-Budget Report speech 1997, *Pre-Budget Report* 1998

Government productivity report: *The Sunday Times*, April 2004

R&D Tax Credit: Institute of Fiscal Studies, *Green Budget 2006*

NHS inflation: *NHS 2010: Reform or Bust*, Reform 2005

Midwives: *Maternity Services in the NHS*, Reform 2005

NHS productivity: "Take Your Pick", *Economist*, 4.3.06

Patient preferences and inhaled insulin: *BioCentury*, Vol. 14, No. 20, 1.5.06

Premature babies as bedblockers: *Sunday Times* 26.3.06

Baumol's Cost Disease: *Performing Arts: The Economic Dilemma*, William J. Baumol and William G. Bowen, Twentieth Century Fund 1966. For recent empirical support across a variety of sectors see "Baumol's Diseases: A Macroeconomic Perspective", William D. Nordhaus, NBER Working Paper 12218, May 2006

European social model: e.g. Martin Wolf, "There is Something Rotten in the Welfare State of Europe", *Financial Times*, 1.3.06

Inequality: Jonathan Shaw, "Inequality under Labour", *Economic Review*, Vol. 23, No. 2

Inequality of Child Trust Fund: Jesse Norman, "A Nice Little Earner if You're Born to Money", *The Times*, 28.8.04

More taxpayers: see the HMRC website, esp. http://www.hmrc.gov.uk/ stats/income_tax/table2_1.pdf

Gordon Brown on Mrs Thatcher and society: *Where There is Greed*, Mainstream Publishing 1989

Chapter 2: It's the society, stupid

Lack of debate over the state: José Harris in *The Boundaries of the State in Modern Britain*, ed. Green and Whiting, Cambridge UP 1996

Communitarians: e.g. Robert Putnam, *Bowling Alone*, Simon and Schuster 2000; Amitai Etzioni, *The Spirit of Community*, Simon and Schuster 1994

Chapter 3: Compassion vs. Conservatism?

Disraeli: see e.g. Smith, P. (1967) *Disraelian Conservatism and Social Reform*. London: Routledge & Kegan Paul

Tory statecraft: Bulpitt, J. (1986) 'The Discipline of the New Democracy: Mrs Thatcher's Domestic Statecraft', *Political Studies*, 34/1

Rival traditions: Greenleaf, W. H. (1983) The British Political Tradition, Vol. 2, *The Ideological Heritage*, pp. 189–358

Chapter 4: Rethinking the basics

Hobbes: *Leviathan*, ed. Macpherson, Penguin 1981

Absolute sovereignty: a fuller treatment would also focus on Locke, who anticipates some of our later discussion with his emphasis on the boundaries of sovereignty, on limited government and on individual rights

Civil and enterprise association: Michael Oakeshott, *On Human Conduct*; see also *The Achievement of Michael Oakeshott*, ed. Jesse Norman, Duckworth 1992, and Auspitz, J.L., "Individuality, Civility, and Theory: The Philosophical Imagination of Michael Oakeshott," *Political Theory* 1976

Philic association: to adapt Aristotle's terms, we can thus contrast philic (connected) association with nomic (law-based, i.e. civil) association and telic (goal-based, i.e. enterprise) association

Chapter 5: Connection and identity

Burke on the little platoons: *Notes on the Revolution in France*. See also David Willetts, *Modern Conservatism*, Penguin 1992

Intermediating institutions: a fuller discussion here would include early 19th Century ideas in France on "intermediary institutions", and the views of Montesquieu, Constant and de Tocqueville

Rule of law: see e.g. A.V. Dicey, *Introduction to the Study of the Law of the Constitution*, Liberty Fund, 1982; and F. Mount, *The British Constitution Now*, Heinemann, 1992

Fellow-feeling: cf. Adam Smith's *Theory of the Moral Sentiments* of 1759, where fellow-feeling or sympathy is a central conception

Friendship: see the third essay in Andrew Sullivan's *Love Undetectable: Notes on Friendship, Sex, and Survival*, Knopf 1998

Marquand: *The Progressive Dilemma: From Lloyd George to Kinnock*, Heinemann 1991, quoting Hirschman's *The Passions and The Interests*

Mount: *Mind the Gap*; see also Peter Gray, "A Brief History of Friendly Societies", Association of Friendly Societies

Hayek on individuals: *Individualism and Economic Order*, University of Chicago Press 1948

Conversation: see Michael Oakeshott, *Rationalism in Politics*, Methuen 1962

Nation State: many writers have discussed the extent to which the nation state is itself changing. cf. Philip Bobbitt, *The Shield of Achilles*, Penguin Books, 2003

Bush's compassionate conservatism: for a more in-depth analysis see also Tim Montgomerie, *Whatever Happened to Compassionate Conservatism?*, Centre for Social Justice, 2004

Funeral Oration: Thucydides, *The History of the Peloponnesian War*, Bk. II

Chapter 6: From identity to policy

de Tocqueville: *Democracy in America*, Book II, Ch. 5

Decentralisation and accountability: see also the "new localism" of Direct
     Democracy (www.direct-democracy.co.uk)

About the authors

Jesse Norman (ww.jessenorman.com) is Executive Director of Policy Exchange. He was a director at Barclays before leaving the City in 1997 to research and teach at University College London. He was educated at Oxford University and at UCL, where he holds an honorary research fellowship in philosophy. His books include *The Achievement of Michael Oakeshott* (ed.), *Breaking the Habits of a Lifetime* and *After Euclid*. He also serves on the advisory council of the Roundhouse, an urban regeneration project for young people in London.

Janan Ganesh is a writer and researcher at Policy Exchange, and for Zac Goldsmith. He was educated at Warwick University and UCL.